UNCA DONALD?
NO PARKING
25¢ PARKING 25¢
'T PLAY WITH YA
I'VE GOT ONLY
NUTES TO MAKE
MATINEE!

A catalog record of this book is available from OCLC and from the BOOM! Studios website, www.boom-studios.com, on the Librarians Page.

BOOM! Studios, 6310 San Vicente Boulevard, Suite 107, Los Angeles, CA 90048-5457. Printed in China. First Printing. ISBN: 978-1-60886-658-8

Disney's

FOUR COLOR ADVENTURES

VOLUME 1

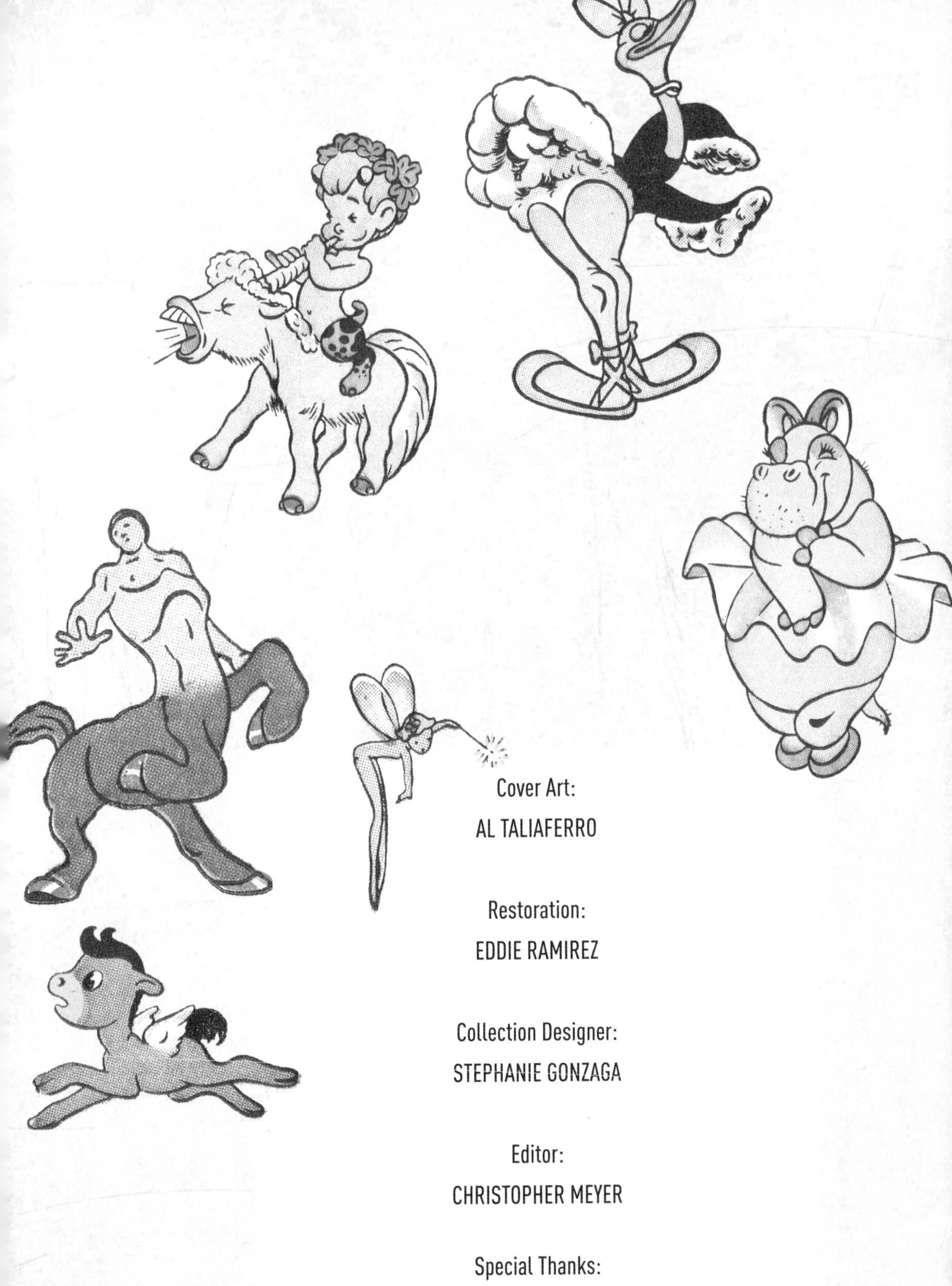

Cover Art:
AL TALIAFERRO

Restoration:
EDDIE RAMIREZ

Collection Designer:
STEPHANIE GONZAGA

Editor:
CHRISTOPHER MEYER

Special Thanks:
JESSE POST, STEVE BEHLING, ROB TOKAR & BRYCE VANKOOTEN OF DISNEY PUBLISHING, DAVID GERSTEIN, THOMAS ANDRAE AND THOMAS JENSEN

AN ADVENTURE IN FOUR COLORS

By David Gerstein

What is a four-color adventure? How would you know one if you had one? Well, keep your hands and arms inside the car—you're having one now. (And you're a cheater if you haven't paid for this book yet. What are you waiting for? Go right to the checkout counter this minute!)

Four Color was Dell Publishing's ongoing one-shot comic. Appearing multiple times per month from 1939 onward, it starred a different character in each issue; sometimes in reprints from newspaper strips, other times in newly-made stories produced just for *Four Color*. Various issues headlined live-action movie stars; radio stars; cartoon stars and comics originals—*Dick Tracy*, still decades from his 1990 Disney movie, was the big name in *Four Color* #1.

Why "Four Color"? In those pre-TV days, print was the dominant news and entertainment medium, and it seems most everyone had a casual understanding of the printing process. "Four color printing" is still the standard method of color printing used today. The press applies four printing plates to each page: one plate for black ink, one for cyan (light blue) ink, one for magenta, and one for yellow. Combinations of those four shades produce the full color spectrum we see on the finished pages. In 1939, when every man and his duck knew this, "Four Color Comics" made for a classy-sounding title.

Disney characters were as popular in 1939 as today; and at the time, Donald Duck—having just acquired his solo cartoon series—was Disney's biggest star. Thus it's no surprise that Don was the headline feature of *Four Color* #4 (1940), Disney's first entry in the series. Mickey Mouse, Donald's predecessor in Disney's hall of fame, would have to wait his turn; oh, for gosh sakes!

Would you believe *Four Color* #4 was the *first* all-color Disney comic book in English? There had been many Disney comic books prior to it, but all had at least some black-and-white pages. (The first one, *Mickey Mouse Series No. 1* [1931], was *all* in black and white.)

Ironically, *Four Color* #4 used its color pages for a formerly black and white product: early *Donald Duck* daily strip gags, drawn by Duck master Al Taliaferro. Ever wonder why Donald's sailor suit is so often black in the comics? It's because Taliaferro—drawing for black and white newspapers—obviously couldn't add blue, so felt a black coat made for better contrast in a monochrome medium. When Western Publishing, Dell's producer/packager, repackaged Taliaferro in *Four Color* and elsewhere, they felt it too much work to erase the black for blue, so they left it as they found it. Then Carl Barks and others carried on the black suit in new color stories, made just for comic books—simply because the Taliaferro reprints had established the tradition.

Four Color #13, the second Disney book in the series, established another tradition. It was Disney's first big movie tie-in comic! And an unusual movie got the focus: *The Reluctant Dragon* (1941), as released to theatres, featured humorist Robert Benchley touring the Disney studio in live action. Cartoon segments such as Goofy's "How to Ride a Horse," the one-shot "Baby Weems," and the featured "Reluctant Dragon" were inserted into the narrative as cartoons-in-progress, screened for Benchley during his tour.

The *Four Color* version of *Dragon* didn't have Benchley, but it did have something new—original Disney comics produced just for comic books! At the time, even *Walt Disney's Comics and Stories* hadn't yet created any original material, so *Four Color* #13 was a first in North America. In later years, editor Chase Craig would recount how these initial stories were produced: by having artists copy film stills and storyboards from the cartoons being adapted. Quite a few scenes in Irving Tripp's "Dragon" adaptation visibly recall poses and even camera angles from the movie—and the same goes for the issue's Donald and Goofy cartoon adaptations.

Four Color would continue to feature frequent Disney issues, and the series became the "test kitchen" of Dell comics: if a character was successful enough in *Four Color* one-shots, he or she could eventually be spun off into his or her own dedicated series, given its own numbering system by counting up the one-shots that had come before.

Mickey got his own title in 1953, with issue #28—after 29 (!) *Four Color* issues that had come before. Donald got his title in 1952, with issue #26—after 30 (!!!) earlier one-shot issues. Goofy, who we presume did the counting, never got a Golden Age title of his own; you commit the crime, you pay the penalty.

It's about time the classic Disney *Four Color* comics were reissued in facsimile—and this volume is just the start. Future editions in this series will feature Barks ducks and Floyd Gottfredson mice just as they were first seen by newsstand-goers—as well as quite a number of surprises that have *never* seen reprint before. Come along and join the club, won't you?

Hmm; if you took our advice and went to the checkout counter before, you're already a member! All together now, members..."M-I-C, K-E-Y—" oh, right. Sorry, Donald. In *Four Color*, you come first. •

David Gerstein's *interest in the Disney Standard Characters began with his childhood viewing of* Plane Crazy *(1928) at a film retrospective. Today David is an animation and comics researcher, writer, and editor working extensively with the Walt Disney Company and its licensees.*

David's published work includes The Floyd Gottfredson Library—Walt Disney's Mickey Mouse: Race to Death Valley *(Fantagraphics 2010); various issues of Boom! Studios'* Uncle Scrooge *(ongoing); and various articles for Disney's* twenty-three *magazine and* D23 *website. David has also worked with Disney in efforts to locate lost* Oswald the Lucky Rabbit *cartoons.*

SERVICE!
HONK!
HONK!

PUTTING COMICS IN CONTEXT

By David Gerstein

Disney comics have always been products of their era—but never more so than in their early days. Everything from the vintage stories' visual milieu to their cultural references bespoke prewar small-town America; or, more precisely, the way small-town America perceived itself, however divorced from reality such perceptions may have been. Characters' language reflected the era: a wallet was also called a "billfold" and shopping was "marketing." Old-time expressions like "doggone it" and "for gosh sakes" were commonplace.

Also commonplace were old-time cultural mores. In the 1930s and 1940s, theatrical cartoons—Disney's included—were aimed largely at an adult cinema audience, and featured story elements we wouldn't see in purely kid-centric animation today. The same elements carried over into the funny pages: slapstick use of firearms, for example, and comedic drinking scenes appeared in Disney stories just as they did in Tom and Jerry. As in all classic cartoons, these scenes were meant as exaggerated fantasy; not as behavior to imitate in daily life.

Of course, for exaggeration, nothing beats prewar pop culture's concept of "the Other": people from cultures outside America's white, gentrified 1930s majority. Fiction was filled with caricatured images of Blacks, Asians, poor whites, Italians, and many others, and Disney comics were not immune. Middle Europeans could be portrayed as oafish, uneducated shop managers; African and island natives were often shown as grass-skirted primitives, speaking either gibberish or an exaggerated Southern dialect.

Stereotypes were seen as a natural element of cartoon shorthand—a means of adding local color with minimal effort. So second-nature were these clichés, in fact, that the comics community's biggest supporters of civil rights—notably Walt Kelly and Theodor "Dr. Seuss" Geisel—used them, too, without considering their impact. It cannot be disputed that closed-minded individuals used negative stereotypes to bolster their prejudices, and that the frequent absence of positive archetypes was demoralizing.

But Disney comics did include some positive archetypes in the old days. Floyd Gottfredson, Carl Barks and other creators did their best to strike a blow for the oppressed, regardless of any other mistakes they made. In this book's "The Reluctant Dragon," for example, the titular character's untraditional behavior and speech patterns could be seen by some as an allegory for alternative lifestyles and changing gender roles. But rather than ridicule the Dragon's behavior or attempt to change it, the protagonists of the story quickly come to accept and celebrate the Dragon for who he is, while the true antagonists of the story are the townspeople who are incapable of looking beyond their own stereotypes.

Though the dated stories in Disney's *Four Color Adventures* sometimes stand as relics of their less enlightened time, we're reprinting them here in the interest of preserving the completeness of these historic comic books—which, regardless of their age, still feature ripping yarns, legendary artwork and large helpings of timeless fun. •

Disney's Four Color Adventures is intended as a "facsimile edition" of the enclosed reprinted material. Every effort has been made to present this material in a manner as close to the original printing as possible, including any art errors and inconsistencies that may have occurred due to the limitations of printing technology in the 1940s. The pages are presented here not only for entertainment purposes, but also in the interest of preserving and exploring the historical context within which they were originally created.

All advertisements in *Four Color* issues #4 and #13 have been reprinted here in their entirety for the sake of archival interest. Please note that all advertised promotions and advertisements within these reprints are no longer valid.

WALT DISNEY'S
DONALD DUCK
10¢
64 PAGES
IN COLOR

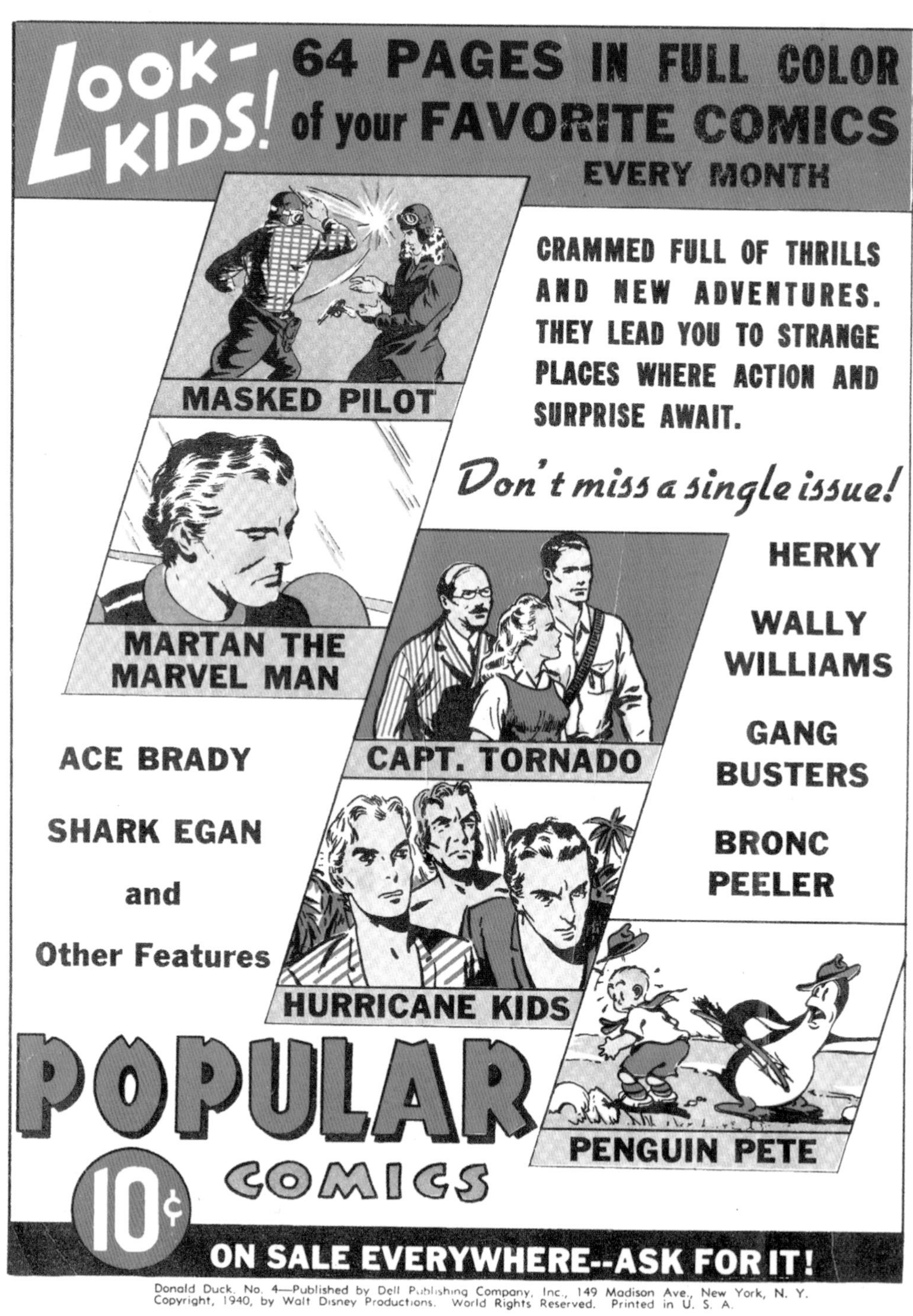

Donald Duck, No. 4—Published by Dell Publishing Company, Inc., 149 Madison Ave., New York, N. Y.

DONALD DUCK

By Walt Disney

DONALD DUCK

By Walt Disney

DONALD DUCK

By Walt Disney

DONALD DUCK

By Walt Disney

DONALD DUCK

By Walt Disney

DONALD DUCK

By Walt Disney

DONALD DUCK

By Walt Disney

DONALD DUCK

By Walt Disney

DONALD DUCK

By Walt Disney

DONALD DUCK

By Walt Disney

DONALD DUCK

By Walt Disney

DONALD DUCK

By Walt Disney

DONALD DUCK

By Walt Disney

DONALD DUCK

By Walt Disney

DONALD DUCK

By Walt Disney

DONALD DUCK

By Walt Disney

DONALD DUCK

By Walt Disney

DONALD DUCK

By Walt Disney

DONALD DUCK

By Walt Disney

DONALD DUCK

By Walt Disney

DONALD DUCK

By Walt Disney

DONALD DUCK

By Walt Disney

DONALD DUCK

By Walt Disney

DONALD DUCK

By Walt Disney

DONALD DUCK

By Walt Disney

DONALD DUCK

By Walt Disney

!

ONE!
SCREECH

NOW SHOWING "TWO GUN GAL"
25¢ UNTIL 1 P.M.
40¢

DONALD DUCK

By Walt Disney

DONALD DUCK

By Walt Disney

DONALD DUCK

By Walt Disney

DONALD DUCK

By Walt Disney

DONAL DUCK

By Walt Disney

DONALD DUCK

By Walt Disney

DONALD DUCK

By Walt Disney

DONALD DUCK

By Walt Disney

DONALD DUCK

By Walt Disney

DONALD DUCK

By Walt Disney

DONALD DUCK

By Walt Disney

DONALD DUCK

By Walt Disney

DONALD DUCK

By Walt Disney

DONALD DUCK

By Walt Disney

DONALD DUCK

By Walt Disney

DONALD DUCK

By Walt Disney

DONALD DUCK

By Walt Disney

I'LL FIX THIS SO YA WON'T USE IT AGAIN!

G'NIGHT, BOYS!

DONALD DUCK

By Walt Disney

DONALD DUCK

By Walt Disney

DONALD DUCK

By Walt Disney

DONALD DUCK

By Walt Disney

DONALD DUCK

By Walt Disney

COSTUME SHOP

I'M GONNA FIX MY DRIVEWAY RIGHT THIS TIME!

R-R-RIP!
CRASH!!
CRACK
?
!

DONALD DUCK

By Walt Disney

DONALD DUCK

By Walt Disney

DONALD DUCK

By Walt Disney

DONALD DUCK

By Walt Disney

DONALD DUCK

By Walt Disney

DONALD DUCK

By Walt Disney

DONALD DUCK

By Walt Disney

DONALD DUCK

By Walt Disney

DONALD DUCK

By Walt Disney

DONALD DUCK

By Walt Disney

DONALD DUCK

By Walt Disney

DONALD DUCK

By Walt Disney

Make a child happy an entire year

SUBSCRIBE
TO THE
MICKEY MOUSE MAGAZINE

A NEW ISSUE EACH MONTH FOR 12 MONTHS COSTS ONLY

$1.00

Postage paid to any address in the U. S. A. and Canada

A year's subscription to this magazine will bring hours of happiness. Walt Disney's beloved Mickey Mouse, Donald Duck and their Pals, the Silly Symphony characters and many others will appear in its pages in delightful stories, games and pictures just as you see them in the movies.

Clip Coupon Below
Enclose $1.00
and Mail as Directed

MICKEY MOUSE MAGAZINE
1270 Sixth Avenue
New York, N. Y.

Enclosed is $1.00. Please send the Mickey Mouse Magazine for one year to:

Name ______________________

Address ______________________

City __________ State __________

If subscription is a gift write your name and address in spaces below and the child will receive a Mickey Mouse gift card with your name on it.

Sign here ______________________

Address ______________________

City __________ State __________

Gift card to read
From ______________________

You Can Make Your Own Records If You Sing Or Play An Instrument

Now a new invention permits you to make a professional-like recording of your own singing, talking or instrument playing. Any one can quickly and easily make phonograph records and play them back at once. Record your voice or your friends' voices. If you play an instrument, you can make a record and you and your friends can hear it as often as you like. You can also record orchestra or favorite radio programs right off the air and replay them whenever you wish.

MAKE YOUR OWN RECORDS AT HOME

Before spending money for an audition, make a "home record" of your voice or musical instrument and mail it to a reliable agency . . . you might be one of the lucky ones to find fame and success through this easy method of bringing your talents before the proper authorities.

IT'S LOTS OF FUN TOO! HAVING RECORDING PARTIES!

You'll get a real thrill out of HOME RECORDING. Surprise your friends by letting them hear your voice or playing right from a record. Record a snappy talking feature. Record jokes and become the life of the party. Great to help train your voice and to cultivate speech. Nothing to practice . . . you start recording at once . . . no other mechanical or electrical devices needed . . . everything necessary included. Nothing else to buy. Just sing, speak or play and HOME RECORDO unit, which operates on any electric or old type phonograph, will do the recording on special blank records we furnish. You can immediately play the records back as often as you wish. Make your home movie a talking picture with HOME RECORDO. Simply make the record while filming and play back while showing the picture.

COMPLETE OUTFIT

INCLUDING SIX TWO-SIDED BLANK RECORDS ONLY **$2.98**

Everything is included. Nothing else to buy and nothing else to pay. You get complete HOME RECORDING UNIT, which includes special recording needle, playing needles, 6 two-sided unbreakable records. Also guide record and spiral feeding attachment and combination recording and playback unit suitable for recording a skit, voice, instrument or radio broadcast. ADDITIONAL 2-SIDED BLANK RECORDS COST ONLY $.75 per dozen.

J.H.W., of Nebraska writes:
Have had wonderful results with Home Recordo so am sending for more blanks. The popularity of Home Recordo at home here has caused a considerable shortage of blank records.

OPERATES ON ANY A.C. OR D.C. ELECTRIC PHONOGRAPHS
RECORD PLAYERS
RADIO-PHONO COMBINATIONS
Old Or New Type PHONOGRAPHS and PORTABLES

A.D.S. of Ohio well pleased and writes:
The Home Recordo unit I just received is proving itself entirely satisfactory. The simplicity with which it operates is remarkable.

HOME RECORDING CO.
Studio DD
11 West 17th Street
New York, N. Y.

SEND NO MONEY! HURRY COUPON! START RECORDING AT ONCE!

HOME RECORDING CO.,
Studio DD, 11 West 17th St.,
New York, N. Y.

Send entire HOME RECORDING OUTFIT (including 6 two-sided records) described above, by return mail. I will pay postman $2.98, plus postage, on arrival. (Send cash or money order now for $3.00 and save postage.)

Send .... additional blank records at $.75 per dozen.

Name ....

Address ....

City & State ....

Note: Canadian and Foreign $3.00 cash with order.

10¢
No. 13
WALT DISNEY'S
Reluctant
Dragon
ALSO
GOOFY
IN
"HOW TO RIDE
A HORSE"
"BABY
WEEMS"
DONALD DUCK
IN
"OLD
MacDONALD
DUCK"
MICKEY MOUSE in "THE SORCERER'S APPRENTICE" from FANTASIA

1

1. Walt Disney's feature picture, "The Reluctant Dragon," combines live-action photography with animated cartoons. It tells the story of Robert Benchley's enthusiasm for Kenneth Grahame's delightful tale about the dragon who wrote poetry. He sets off for the Disney Studios to convince Walt Disney that he should make a moving picture based on the dragon story.

2

2. On his way to Walt Disney's office, Benchley gets lost in the many buildings on the Disney lot. With the help of Frances Gifford, he makes a tour of the unusual departments connected with the making of Disney pictures. Here they are in the model department, where figures of the many Disney characters are sculptured.

3

3. Ward Kimball, one of Walt Disney's top animators, shows Robert Benchley what makes Disney characters move.

WALT DISNEY'S RELUCTANT DRAGON, No. 13-PUBLISHED BY DELL PUBLISHING COMPANY, INC.

149 Madison Ave., New York, N. Y.

WALT DISNEY'S

Reluctant Dragon

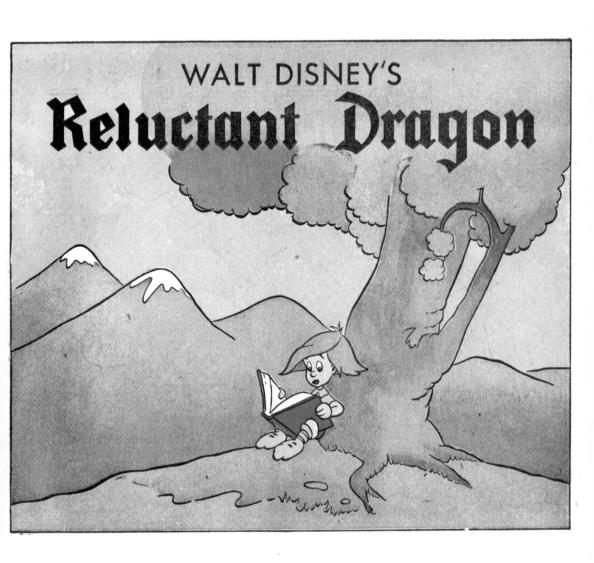

LONG AGO - IT MIGHT HAVE BEEN HUNDREDS OF YEARS AGO- THERE WAS A SHEPHERD WHO LIVED IN A LITTLE COTTAGE WITH HIS WIFE AND YOUNG SON. THE BOY, WHEN HE WAS NOT HELPING HIS FATHER, SPENT MOST OF HIS TIME READING BOOKS.

ONE DAY HE WAS SITTING UNDER A TREE READING, WHEN HIS FATHER RUSHED UP ALL OUT OF BREATH.

"THEN UP RODE SIR HUBERT ON HIS MILKY-WHITE STEED, 'FEAR YOU NOT FAIR MAIDEN,' QUOTH HE—"

IT'S 'ORRIBLE SON-'ORRIBLE! I'SEEN IT/ 'ARFWAY OUT OF 'IS 'OLE'E WAS-COVERED WITH SCALES AND SUCH LIKE-AN'A TAIL WITH SORT OF 'OOK ON IT.

IT'S ONLY A DRAGON, FATHER, ONLY A DRAGON. DON'T WORRY, I'LL HAVE A LOOK AT HIM AS SOON AS I'VE FINISHED READING THIS CHAPTER.

THE BOY WAS NOT EVEN EXCITED ABOUT THE NEWS OF A FEROCIOUS MONSTER IN THE NEIGHBORHOOD. HE READ ABOUT SO MANY STRANGE THINGS IN HIS BOOKS THAT A MERE DRAGON, EVEN ONE WITH SCALES AND A HOOK ON HIS TAIL, WAS NOTHING SPECIAL.

HIS FATHER DASHED OFF TO WARN THE VILLAGERS OF THE DANGER, WHILE THE BOY WENT ON READING.

I GUESS THIS MUST BE THE DRAGON'S CAVE ALL RIGHT.
WHAT'S THAT? IT SOUNDS LIKE SINGING TO ME
THE BOY PEERED INSIDE THE CAVE AND SAW THE DRAGON TAKING A BATH AND SINGING HAPPILY TO HIMSELF.
Mi-mi-mi-mi! LA-La la-la la-la LA-la! Mi-mi-mi!
THERE WAS NOTHING TO BE AFRAID OF, SO THE BOY STEPPED INSIDE.
AHEM- HELLO! HELLO, DRAGON-
WHAT- WHO'S THAT?

BUT THE BOY EXPLAINED THAT HE HAD JUST DROPPED IN FOR A FRIENDLY CHAT.

THE DRAGON ASKED THE BOY TO TURN THE OTHER WAY WHILE HE FINISHED HIS BATH.

AS HE SAT THERE THE BOY TRIED TO START A FRIENDLY CONVERSATION.

THE BOY DECIDED THE DRAGON MUST HAVE BEEN BUSY DEVOURING FAIR DAMSELS, BUT THE DRAGON DENIED EVER DOING SUCH THINGS.

THE DRAGON GOT UP AND STARTED TO DANCE AROUND IN A MOST UNDRAGON-LIKE MANNER.
YOU'LL LOVE THIS – I CALL IT "JUST A-DRIFTING" JUST A-DRIFTING O'ER THE LEA, LIKE A DEWDROP, FANCY FREE, PLAYING WITH THE GENTLE BREEZES ROMPING WITH THE BUMBLE BEEZES. OH WHAT FUN – JOY NEVER CEASES JUST A-DRIFTING —
VERY NICE, VERY NICE! BUT WAIT A MINUTE! I'VE GOT SOMETHING SERIOUS TO TELL YOU YOU'RE IN FOR SOME TROUBLE!

THE DRAGON HATED TO INTERRUPT HIS POEM IN THE MIDDLE, BUT HE HAD TO FIND OUT WHAT THE BOY MEANT.

THE BOY EXPLAINED THAT ALL THE VILLAGERS THOUGHT DRAGONS WERE HORRIBLE BEASTS THAT OUGHT TO BE DONE AWAY WITH!

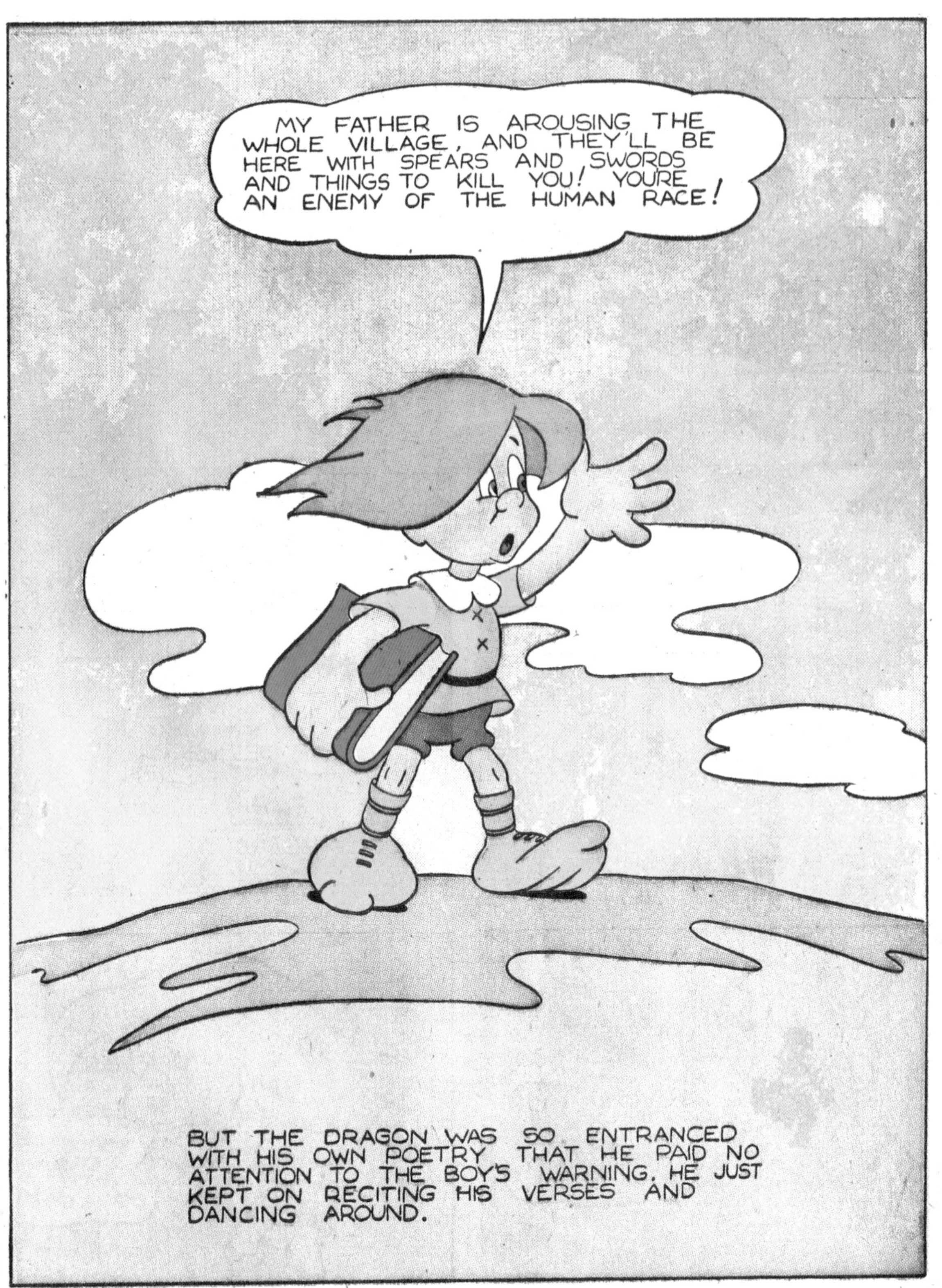
MY FATHER IS AROUSING THE WHOLE VILLAGE, AND THEY'LL BE HERE WITH SPEARS AND SWORDS AND THINGS TO KILL YOU! YOU'RE AN ENEMY OF THE HUMAN RACE!
BUT THE DRAGON WAS SO ENTRANCED WITH HIS OWN POETRY THAT HE PAID NO ATTENTION TO THE BOY'S WARNING. HE JUST KEPT ON RECITING HIS VERSES AND DANCING AROUND.

SKIPPING, TRIPPING HERE AND THERE,
HITHER, THITHER, EVERYWHERE,
TOPSY-TURVY, WILLY-NILLY,
LIKE A SILLY DAFFY DILLY,
JUST A-DRIFTING.

OH, IF YOU WON'T BE SENSIBLE, I'M GOING HOME. I WARNED YOU, ANYWAY

WHAT'S GOING ON? WHY ALL THE CROWDS, I WONDER

HEY, WHAT'S ALL THE EXCITMENT? A PARADE?

WHEN HE GOT TO THE VILLAGE, THE BOY SAW CROWDS LINING THE STREET. HE CALLED TO TWO OF HIS FRIENDS WHO HAD A GOOD VIEW FROM A TREE.

THE BOY HEARD THE CROWDS BEGIN TO SHOUT AND CHEER FOR SOMEONE COMING DOWN THE STREET.

THE BOY STUCK HIS HEAD BETWEEN THE LEGS OF A MAN IN THE FRONT OF THE CROWD. HE LOOKED UP AND DOWN THE STREET BUT COULD NOT SEE ANYTHING YET. THEN HE HEARD THE TRAMP OF A GREAT WAR HORSE COMING DOWN THE COBBLED STREET. THE CHEERS OF THE CROWDS SWELLED TO A MIGHTY SHOUT AS THE FAMOUS KNIGHT CAME NEARER. THE BOY FELT HIS HEART BEAT FASTER WITH EXCITEMENT AND FOUND HIMSELF CHEERING WITH THE OTHERS, AS HE CAUGHT A GLIMPSE OF THE GREAT SIR GILES.

BLIMEY. 'E'S A SPECTACLE 'E IS!
'OORAY, 'OORAY FOR SIR GILES!
'OORAY FOR SIR GILES! 'OORAY FOR THE DRAGON-KILLER
AIN'T 'E GRAND?
THE KNIGHT WAS THE MOST MAGNIFICENT THING THE BOY HAD EVER SEEN. HIS ARMOR WAS INLAID WITH GOLD, AND HIS HELMET HAD A BEAUTIFUL WHITE PLUME WAVING FROM THE TOP. THE BOY SAW THE KNIGHT STOP IN FRONT OF THE INN AND DISMOUNT AS THE VILLAGERS CROWDED AROUND. SIR GILES TOLD THE PEOPLE THAT THEY NEED NOT WORRY ANY MORE. HE, THE GREAT DRAGON-KILLER, HAD COME TO SLAY THE DREADFUL MONSTER WHICH HAD SCOURGED THE COUNTRYSIDE
GOSH-ISN'T HE WONDERFUL?

THEN THE BOY REMEMBERED HIS FRIEND, THE DRAGON, WHO REALLY WAS NOT A DREADFUL MONSTER AT ALL. THE BOY THOUGHT SIR GILES WAS WONDERFUL, AND HE WOULD RATHER SEE A GOOD BATTLE BETWEEN A KNIGHT AND A DRAGON THAN ANYTHING IN THE WORLD. BUT STILL– THE DRAGON WAS A NICE SORT OF FELLOW---

THE BOY FOUND THE DRAGON SITTING UNDER A TREE PLAYING HIS FLUTE AND TEACHING SOME BIRDS A NEW TUNE.

HE WAS SO PLEASED WITH HIS NEW MELODY THAT HE DID NOT NOTICE THE BOY AT FIRST.

THE DRAGON PAID NO ATTENTION TO THE BOY'S NEWS APPARENTLY NOT REALIZING HOW IMPORTANT IT WAS

THE BOY SHOUTED HIS WARNING AT THE TOP OF HIS LUNGS, BUT HE GOT NO RESPONSE.

THE DRAGON JUST WOULD NOT BE WORRIED. HE CALMLY WENT ON WITH HIS SINGING LESSON TO THE BIRDS.

THE BOY WALKED BACK TO THE VILLAGE WORRYING ABOUT THE BAD FIX THE DRAGON WAS IN.. A FIGHT WOULD BE NICE, BUT---

THE BOY DID NOT KNOW WHAT HE WOULD SAY TO SIR GILES, BUT HE HAD TO TRY SOMETHING.

AS HE LOOKED AROUND THE DOOR HE HEARD THE SOUND OF SPLASHING WATER.

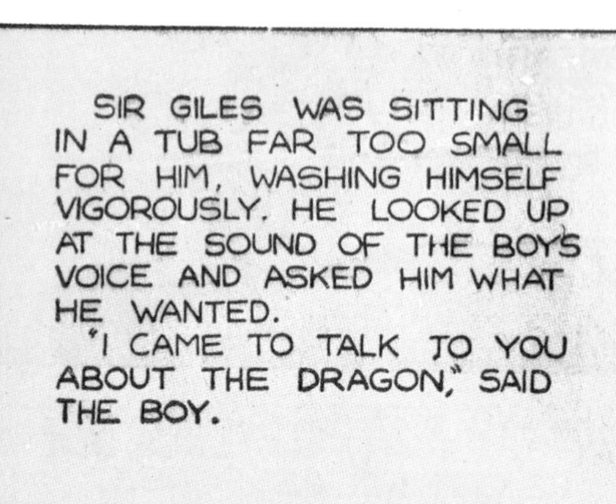

SIR GILES WAS SITTING IN A TUB FAR TOO SMALL FOR HIM, WASHING HIMSELF VIGOROUSLY. HE LOOKED UP AT THE SOUND OF THE BOY'S VOICE AND ASKED HIM WHAT HE WANTED.
"I CAME TO TALK TO YOU ABOUT THE DRAGON," SAID THE BOY.

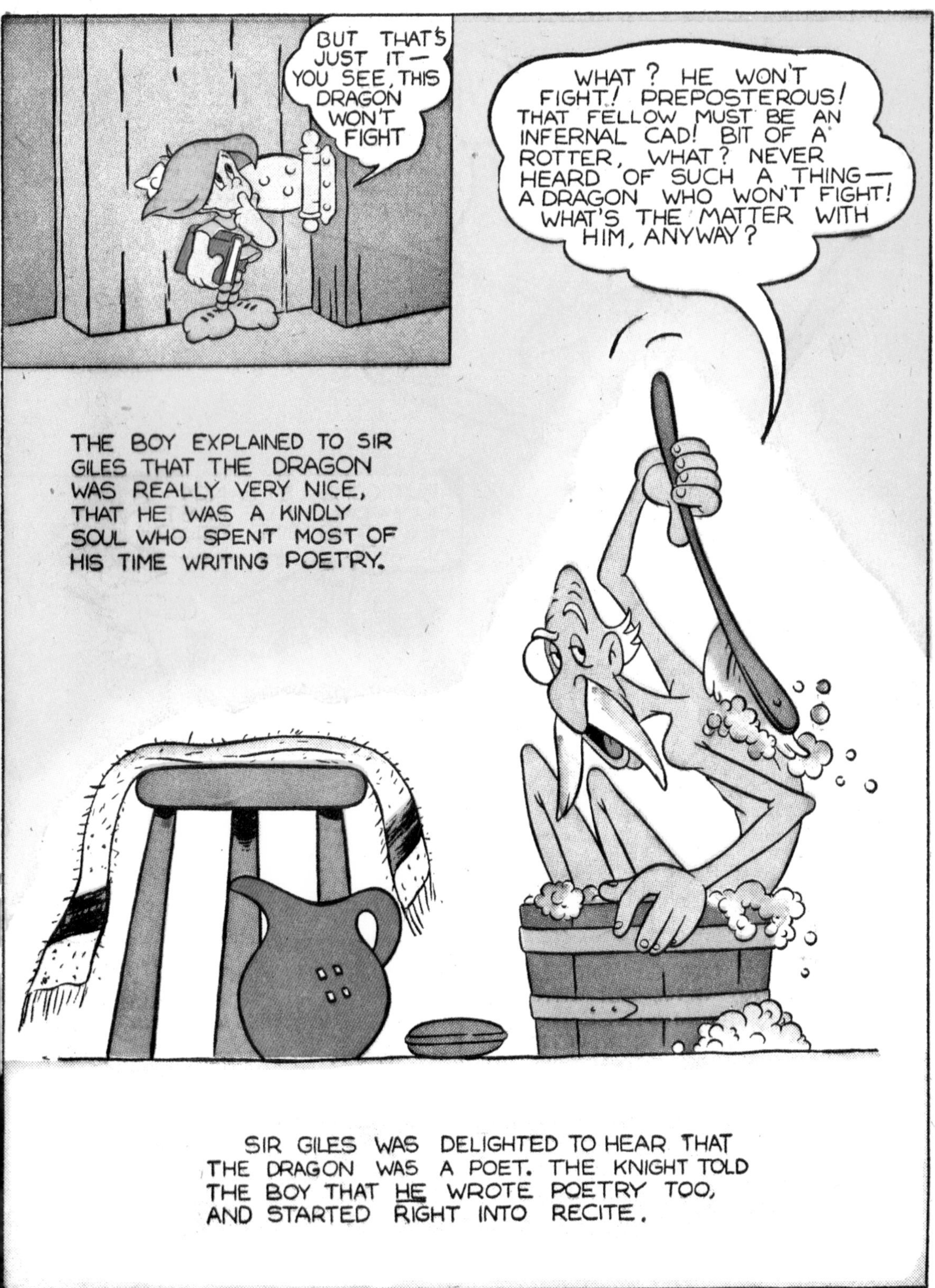
BUT THAT'S JUST IT— YOU SEE, THIS DRAGON WON'T FIGHT
WHAT? HE WON'T FIGHT! PREPOSTEROUS! THAT FELLOW MUST BE AN INFERNAL CAD! BIT OF A ROTTER, WHAT? NEVER HEARD OF SUCH A THING— A DRAGON WHO WON'T FIGHT! WHAT'S THE MATTER WITH HIM, ANYWAY?
THE BOY EXPLAINED TO SIR GILES THAT THE DRAGON WAS REALLY VERY NICE, THAT HE WAS A KINDLY SOUL WHO SPENT MOST OF HIS TIME WRITING POETRY.
SIR GILES WAS DELIGHTED TO HEAR THAT THE DRAGON WAS A POET. THE KNIGHT TOLD THE BOY THAT HE WROTE POETRY TOO, AND STARTED RIGHT INTO RECITE.

YOU'VE NO DOUBT HEARD OF MY "ODE TO A FLEECY CLOUD" IT GOES—
OH FLEECY CLOUD, OH CLOUD OF FLEECE, UP IN THE SKY SO HIGH OH—— OH MY—
BUT COME, LET'S NOT DILLY-DALLY! WE MUST MEET THIS FINE FELLOW AT ONCE.
SIR GILES QUICKLY DRESSED HIMSELF AND WENT OUT WITH THE BOY TOWARD THE DRAGON'S CAVE. ALTHOUGH THE KNIGHT SEEMED INTERESTED IN MEETING THE DRAGON BECAUSE HE WROTE POETRY, THE BOY MADE HIM PROMISE TO DISCUSS THE FIGHT.
AT THE CAVE THEY FOUND THE DRAGON EATING
A DRAGON POET! HOW JOLLY THIS WILL BE!
Sir Giles

THE DRAGON WAS VERY FRIENDLY AND AND WELCOMED BOTH HIS VISITORS.

THE BOY AND THE KNIGHT CLIMBED UP ON THE DRAGON'S BODY AND SAT.

THE BOY COULD SEE THAT THE DRAGON WAS STILL NOT THE LEAST BIT WORRIED ABOUT HIS GREAT DANGER.

HE WAS INTERESTED ONLY IN ENJOYING HIMSELF AND SHOWING HIS GUESTS A GOOD TIME.

THE BOY DID NOT PAY MUCH ATTENTION TO ALL THE POLITE CONVERSATION. HE WAS WORRIED ABOUT THAT FIGHT.

THE KNIGHT DID NOT CATCH ON! ALL HE WAS INTERESTED IN WAS POETRY, IT SEEMED.

WHILE THE DRAGON RECITED, THE BOY FIDGETED, ANXIOUS TO HAVE THE DRAGON AND THE KNIGHT SETTLE THE FIGHT MATTER.

THE KNIGHT SAT ENTRANCED APPARENTLY NOT THINKING THAT THIS DRAGON WAS A MONSTER HE WAS SUPPOSED TO SLAY.

THIS GENTLE, POETRY-LOVING KNIGHT BEGAN TO LOOK LESS AND LESS LIKE A GREAT DRAGON-KILLER

THE BOY BEGAN TO GET JUST AS ANNOYED AT SIR GILES AS AT THE DRAGON.

THE PLEASANT PICNIC IS THROWN INTO A PANIC BY THE BOY'S POEM.

THE KNIGHT AGREES WITH THE BOY AND THEY BOTH ARGUE WITH THE DRAGON.

THE DRAGON IS NO LONGER A BIT FRIENDLY TO SIR GILES AND THE BOY.

HE STALKS AWAY INDIGNANTLY INTO HIS CAVE, LEAVING THEM OUTSIDE.

THE DRAGON HAS BEEN LISTENING TO THEIR TALK AND COMES OUT OF HIS CAVE.
THE DRAGON APPEARS, WHAT A BEAUTIFUL SIGHT WITH HIS SCALES ALL AGLEAM IN THE DAWN'S EARLY LIGHT!
NOW REALLY! YOU'RE JUST FLATTERING ME.
NO, OLD FELLOW– IT'S TRUE! A BEAUTIFUL DAMSEL THROWS FLOWERS AT YOU!

AT ME! HOO! HOO!
LOOK! HERE COMES SIR GILES ON HIS MILKY-WHITE HORSE.

THE DRAGON CATCHES THE SPIRIT OF THINGS AS THE BOY AND THE KNIGHT DESCRIBE THE IMAGINARY FIGHT.

HIS BRAVE BATTLE-CRY HE'S YELLING, OF COURSE?

THEY ALL GET AS EXCITED AS IF THEY WERE WITNESSING THE GLORIOUS BATTLE

AS I RAMP AND I ROAR, I CUT QUITE A FIGGER!

SIC SEMPER TYRANNUS TALLY-HO AND PRO-TEM YOICKS, TEMPUS FUGIT AND CHERCHEZ LA FEMME!

THE BOY'S MENTION OF A SPEAR SUDDENLY BROUGHT THE DRAGON BACK TO REALITY. HE DECIDED ONCE MORE THAT HE WOULD NOT FIGHT, THAT HE DID NOT WANT TO GET HURT.
BUT THE KNIGHT HAD AN IDEA AND WHISPERED INTO THE DRAGON'S EAR. THE DRAGON LOOKED PLEASED.

HE HAD SOME SUGGESTIONS FOR THE KNIGHT, WHILE THE BOY CRANED HIS NECK TO LISTEN TO THEIR PLANS.

THE DRAGON WANTED TO BE SURE THAT THEIR LITTLE IDEA WOULD BE HONEST AND RESPECTABLE.

SIR GILES AND THE BOY WALKED BACK TO THE VILLAGE, WHILE THE DRAGON CHUCKLED TO HIMSELF ABOUT THE PLAN FOR A FIGHT THAT WOULD ONLY LOOK LIKE A FIGHT. IT WOULD MAKE THE VILLAGERS HAPPY, BUT NO ONE WOULD GET HURT.

BUT MAYBE HE WOULD GET HURT! MAYBE THE PLAN WOULD NOT GO JUST AS THEY PLANNED IT. ONCE MORE THE DRAGON WAS AFRAID.

SO THE DRAGON SPENT MOST OF THE NIGHT WORRYING. HE WAS STILL WORRIED THE NEXT DAY AS THE CROWDS GATHERED FOR THE FIGHT.

THE VILLAGERS WERE DRESSED IN THEIR SUNDAY CLOTHES AND THEY CARRIED LUNCH BASKETS WITH FOOD AND WITH BOTTLES STICKING OUT OF THEM.

THEY ALL SCRAMBLED FOR THE BEST SEATS AS THE TRUMPETS ANNOUNCED THAT EVERYTHING WAS ALMOST READY. BUT INSIDE THE DRAGON'S CAVE, THINGS WERE FAR FROM READY.

NO MATTER HOW HARD HE TRIED THE DRAGON COULD NOT WORK UP ANY MORE THAN A TINY PUFF OF SMOKE.

HE LOOKED AT THE BOY APOLOGETICALLY. THE FIGHT REALLY WOULD NOT BE ANY GOOD UNLESS THE DRAGON BREATHED FIRE. IT JUST WOULD NOT LOOK RIGHT. THE BOY WAS DISGUSTED.

"TOO BAD YOU'RE NOT A REAL DRAGON INSTEAD OF A PUNK POET."

THE DRAGON PICKED UP HIS EARS. HE LOOKED ANGRY. SMOKE AND FLAMES CAME POURING FROM HIS MOUTH.

THE BOY WAS DELIGHTED AND REPEATED HIS INSULTING REMARK OVER AND OVER AS THE FLAMES GREW. NEVER BEFORE HAD THE DRAGON BREATHED SUCH FIRE AND SMOKE.

OUTSIDE, THE VILLAGERS SHUDDERED WITH DELIGHT AT THE IDEA OF SUCH A FEROCIOUS DRAGON.

THE DRAGON WAS A FEARSOME SIGHT AS THE INSULTING WORDS LASHED AT HIM. THE BOY WAS DELIGHTED! SO WAS THE DRAGON. HE WAS BEGINNING TO LIKE THE IDEA OF BEING FIERCE AND TERRIBLE. HE WOULD SHOW THOSE VILLAGERS A BATTLE THEY WOULD NEVER FORGET.

OUTSIDE, THE PEOPLE, GLANCING NERVOUSLY AT THE MOUTH OF THE DRAGON'S CAVE, KEPT LOOKING FOR THE KNIGHT. SOON HE APPEARED ON THE CREST OF THE HILL AND RODE SLOWLY FORTH ON THE GREEN LEVEL SPACE WHICH STRETCHED UP TO THE MOUTH OF THE CAVE. HIS GOLDEN ARMOR GLEAMED IN THE SUN. HIS GREAT SPEAR WAS HELD ERECT, THE LITTLE WHITE PENNON, CRIMSON-CROSSED, FLUTTERED FROM ITS POINT. SIR GILES DREW REIN AND STOOD MOTIONLESS.

FROM THE CAVE CAME A ROAR, A BELLOW, AND MORE FLAMES AND SMOKE, OUT OF WHICH DASHED THE DRAGON.

SIC SEMPER TYRANNUS TALLY-HO AND PRO-TEM. YOICKS, TEMPUS FUGIT, AND CHERCHEZ LA FÉMME! READY OR NOT, HERE I COME!

SIR GILES LOWERED HIS SPEAR, AIMED IT AT THE DRAGON AND SPURRED HIS HORSE. THE WHITE STEED PAWED THE EARTH, GROWLED AND SNORTED, LOWERED HIS HEAD AND CHARGED. BUT WHEN THEY REACHED THE SPOT WHERE THE DRAGON HAD BEEN, HE WAS NOT THERE ANY MORE. SHOUTING "BOO! BOO!" TO FRIGHTEN THE CROWD, HE HAD LAID DOWN A SMOKE SCREEN AND DASHED BEHIND A BIG ROCK. THE KNIGHT LOOKED AROUND FOR HIM.

YOO, HOO! HERE I AM!

STOP ACTING SILLY, OLD BOY. THIS IS SERIOUS BUSINESS, Y'KNOW. COME NOW, I'LL CHASE YOU!
HELP, HELP, OH HELP!
SIR GILES! SIR GILES! WHERE ARE YOU!
RIGHT HERE, YOU BLIGHTER! NOT QUITE SO MUCH SMOKE, IF YOU PLEASE!
YOICKS! TARANTARA! TARANTARA!
OH DEAR! HELP! GRACIOUS! HELP! HELP!
GRRRRR!

THE DELIGHTED CROWD HEARD WHAT SEEMED TO BE A VIOLENT BATTLE. GROANS AND SHOUTS AND CRIES FOR HELP ISSUED FROM THE CAVE. BUT INSIDE, THE BOY WAS SEEING SOMETHING VERY DIFFERENT FROM A FIGHT TO THE DEATH. THE DRAGON AND THE KNIGHT BANGED AND SHOUTED FOR THE BENEFIT OF THE CROWD, BUT THE DRAGON GOT BUSY PREPARING TEA AT THE SAME TIME.

THE DRAGON OBLIGINGLY RAN OUT OF THE CAVE WITH THE ENTHUSIASTIC KNIGHT AT HIS HEELS. THE CROWD ROARED ITS APRROVAL, SHOUTING ENCOURAGEMENT TO SIR GILES, AS THE END OF THE FIGHT DREW NEAR. IT WAS OBVIOUS THAT THE FRIGHTENED DRAGON COULD NOT HOLD OUT MUCH LONGER.
SHOW A LITTLE FIGHT, OLD BOY! DON'T MAKE THIS LOOK TOO EASY FOR ME.
HOW'S THIS? SNORT! BELLOW! GROWL!
SORRY, OLD CHAP, THE TIME HAS COME, Y'KNOW. LET'S MAKE IT GOOD.
YOU MEAN I DIE NOW!

WITH A LAST DESPERATE YELL, THE DRAGON ROLLED OVER ON THE GROUND, TREMBLING AND QUIVERING AS IF IN THE LAST AGONIES OF A TERRIBLE DEATH. SIR GILES PLACED HIS FOOT ON THE DRAGON'S NECK, TOOK OFF HIS HELMET AND SMILED AND BOWED TO THE CHEERS OF THE CROWD.

THE DEATH SCENE WAS VERY REALISTIC, SO MUCH SO THAT THE BOY WAS WORRIED.

AH, YA-AS, INDEED! THANK YOU, THANK YOU. IT WAS A HARD BATTLE, HE PUT UP A GOOD FIGHT!

THE CROWD GATHERED AROUND ADMIRINGLY

"BAIN'T YOU GOIN' TO CUT 'IS 'EAD ORF, MASTER?" ASKED ONE OF THE APPLAUDING VILLAGERS.

"WELL, NOT TODAY, I THINK," REPLIED SIR GILES PLEASANTLY. "YOU SEE, THAT CAN BE DONE AT ANY TIME. THERE'S NO HURRY. I'LL GIVE HIM A GOOD TALKING TO, AND YOU'LL FIND HE'LL BE A VERY DIFFERENT DRAGON."

IT SEEMED A GOOD TIME TO EAT, SO ALL THE BASKETS WERE OPENED AND THE PICNIC BEGAN. SIR GILES AND THE DRAGON AND THE BOY JOINED IN, AND EVERYONE HAD A JOLLY TIME.

AFTER REFRESHMENTS, SIR GILES MADE A SPEECH, IN WHICH HE INFORMED THE AUDIENCE THAT HE HAD REMOVED THEIR DIREFUL SCOURGE, AT A GREAT DEAL OF TROUBLE AND INCONVENIENCE TO HIMSELF, AND NOW THEY WERE NOT TO GO ABOUT GRUMBLING AND FANCYING THEY HAD GOT GRIEVANCES BECAUSE THEY HAD NONE. THEN HE TOLD THEM THAT THE DRAGON HAD BEEN THINKING THINGS OVER, AND SAW THERE WERE TWO SIDES TO EVERY QUESTION, AND HE WAS NOT GOING TO DO IT ANY MORE; AND IF THEY WERE GOOD PERHAPS HE WOULD STAY AND SETTLE DOWN THERE. SO THEY MUST ALL MAKE FRIENDS - THE CROWD APPLAUDED, AND THEY CHEERED THE KNIGHT AND THE DRAGON AND THE BOY.

IT WAS BEGINNING TO GROW LATE WHEN THE VILLAGERS STARTED PACKING THEIR BASKETS TO GO HOME. THE KNIGHT AND THE DRAGON AND THE BOY, HOWEVER, STARTED BACK TO THE CAVE. THE LIGHTS IN THE LITTLE VILLAGE BEGAN TO GO OUT, BUT THERE WERE STARS AND A LATE MOON. AS THEY CLIMBED THE HILL TOGETHER, THE POETIC SPELL OF THE NIGHT TOOK HOLD OF THEM. THEY RECITED POETRY.
OH MOON OF CHEESE
OH CHEESY MOON –
UP IN THE SKY SO CLEAR-
OH – OH DEAR.
BEAUTIFUL, SIMPLY BEAUTIFUL.
AS THEY TURNED THE LAST CORNER AND DISAPPEARED FROM VIEW, SNATCHES OF AN OLD SONG WERE BORNE BACK ON THE NIGHT BREEZE. ONE OF THEM WAS SINGING, AND IT SEEMED TO BE THE DRAGON!

TO BEGIN WITH, MR. JOHN WEEMS WAS A PERFECTLY ORDINARY INDIVIDUAL------

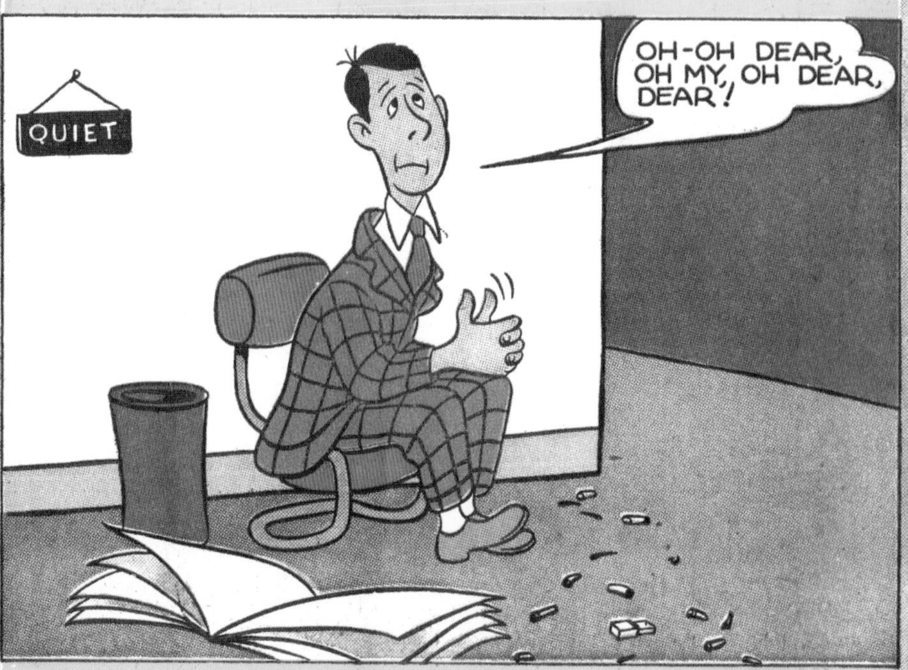

WHO FOUND HIMSELF IN THE ORDINARY SITUATION OF WAITING TO BECOME A FATHER.

WHEN AN ORDINARY-LOOKING NURSE MADE HER ORDINARY AND CONVENTIONAL ANNOUNCEMENT.

MR. WEEMS HAD WHAT IS GENERALLY CONSIDERED THE ORDINARY REACTION.

TWO NIGHTS LATER A NURSE, ON HER ORDINARY ROUNDS, MADE AN ORDINARY REMARK TO ONE OF HER CHARGES, BABY WEEMS.

THE BABY'S ANSWER WAS IN PERFECT AND DISTINCT ENGLISH, BUT THE NURSE DID NOT BOTHER TO WEIGH THE MEANING OF HIS WORDS.

SHE SIMPLY FAINTED DEAD AWAY. THEN FOR THE NEXT FEW MINUTES THE HOSPITAL, CONFRONTED WITH A MIRACLE, WAS FULL OF AMAZING HUMANITY.

THE DOCTOR AND SPECIALISTS CAME AND PONDERED WONDERED, EXAMINED, AND CONSULTED, BUT ALL THEY COULD TELL THE STARTLED WORLD WAS THAT THE TWO-DAY-OLD BABY REALLY DID TALK!

IN NO TIME AT ALL, THE GENTLEMEN OF THE PRESS WERE SWARMING AROUND WITH THE HOTTEST PIECE OF NEWS SINCE THE DELUGE.

MR. AND MRS. WEEMS WERE A LITTLE BIT FRIGHTENED AT IT ALL, BUT WERE STILL VERY HAPPY IN THEIR PARENTHOOD – EVEN IF THEY DIDN'T GET TO SEE THEIR BABY VERY OFTEN.

MEANWHILE, BABY WEEMS, WHOSE UNCANNY ABILITY TO TALK WAS MATCHED BY A MENTAL DEVELOPMENT EQUALLY ASTOUNDING, WAS STUDYING THE COMPLEXITIES OF THE ATOM.

BETWEEN CHANGES HE PURSUED HIS STUDIES, DISCUSSED WEIGHT PROBLEMS WITH THE FINEST MINDS OF THE WORLD.

FOR RELAXATION HE TROUNCED THE MASTER CHESS PLAYER OF THE WORLD. HE SHOWED THE SOFTER SIDE OF HIS NATURE BY COMPOSING MUSIC.

I MUST FINISH THIS NEW OPERA FOR THE METROPOLITAN TODAY - THEY WANT TO START REHEARSALS TOMORROW.

HE CONDUCTED HIS OWN SYMPHONY ORCHESTRA BEFORE HUGE AUDIENCES WHICH ROARED THEIR APPLAUSE FOR THE WORLD'S NEW HERO.

THE REST OF PLODDING HUMANITY GOT IN ON THE FRINGES OF GLORY IN THE USUAL MANNER. BABY WEEMS INSPIRED ALL THE NEW STYLES.

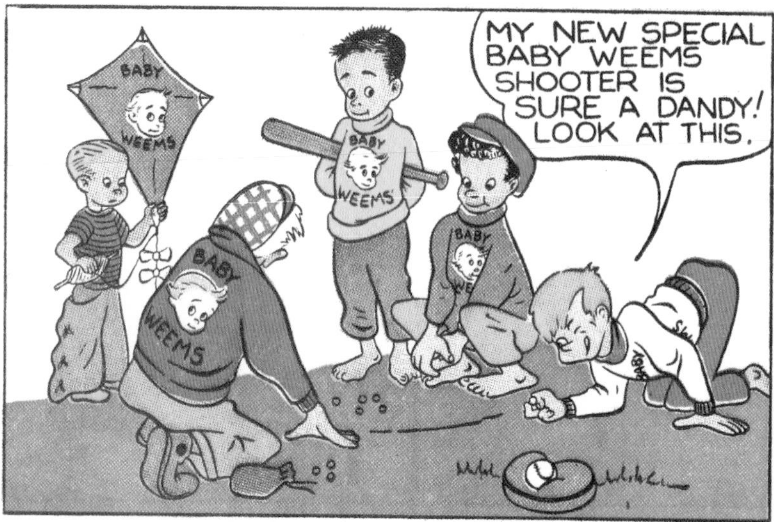

MY NEW SPECIAL BABY WEEMS SHOOTER IS SURE A DANDY! LOOK AT THIS.

WEEM'S BEACH WEAR

HONORS OF ALL KINDS WERE HEAPED ON HIS TINY SHOULDERS BY AN ADORING WORLD.

HE ACCEPTED THESE HONORS GRAVELY AND GRACIOUSLY NO MATTER WHERE THEY CAME FROM.

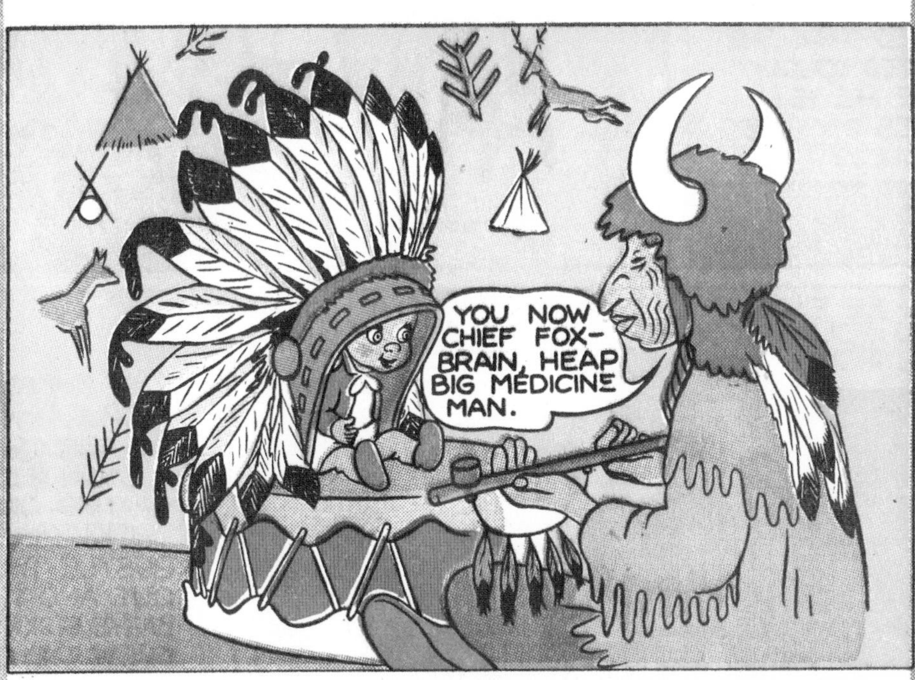

HE BECAME, IN TURN, A LEGIONNAIRE OF HONOR, AND A KNIGHT OF THE GARTER, SIR HERBERT WEEMS. FAMOUS ARTISTS PAINTED HIS PORTRAITS AND........

SCULPTORS IMMORTALIZED HIM IN STONE. BUT TO TWO PEOPLE HE WAS STILL JUST "OUR BABY," EVEN THOUGH THEY HEARD HIS VOICE ONLY WHEN HE SPOKE OVER THE RADIO.

THE ONLY TIME THEY EVER SAW HIM NOW WAS IN THE NEWSREELS. ONCE, IN THE THEATER, MRS. WEEMS GREW SO EXCITED THAT SHE SHOUTED LOUDLY "THERE HE IS!! THERE'S MY BABY, MY BABY!"

HE SOUNDS TIRED POOR DEAR.
MR. CHAIRMAN LADIES AND GENTLEMAN

THAT'LL BE ENOUGH OUT OF YOU FOLKS! COME ALONG, NOW!
EXIT
BUT I TELL YOU HE IS MY BABY!

THE THEATER PEOPLE, THINKING THEY HAD A COUPLE OF CRANKS ON THEIR HANDS, BUSTLE THEM OUT AND THEIR BABY'S SUCCESSES GREW AND GREW EVERY DAY.

PROBLEM AFTER PROBLEM WAS SOLVED BY THE "WONDER BABE" UNTIL IT WAS FELT HE COULD ANSWER ANY QUESTION!

AND THEN ONE DAY, WORD CAME TO THE CAPITOL THAT IN RESPONSE TO THE THOUSANDS OF LETTERS, BABY WEEMS WOULD PUBLICLY ANSWER THE PROBLEM, HOW TO FIND HAPPINESS!

HIS TRIP THROUGH THE ROARING CITY WAS AN UNENDING TRIUMPH. AMONG THE MILLIONS WHO CHEERED THEMSELVES HOARSE WAS MR. AND MRS. WEEMS.

LATER THAT DAY, THE WORLD SAT NEAR IT'S RADIOS WAITING TO HEAR THE WORDS THAT WOULD BRING THE GOLDEN AGE - BUT SOMETHING HAPPENED.

THE HEARTS OF MILLIONS OF PEOPLE STOOD STILL AND AT HOME, MR. AND MRS. WEEMS, REMEMBERING THEIR BABY'S APPEARANCE, FELT A SUDDEN FEAR!

YES, SOMETHING WAS INDEED WRONG! BUT EVEN NOW, WHILE THE TINY FLAME OF LIFE FLICKERED UNCERTAINLY, THE DISTRAUGHT PARENTS WERE DENIED ADMISSION TO THEIR BABY'S BEDSIDE.

ALL OVER THE WORLD, CROWDS STOOD DUMBLY IN THE RAIN UNDER LOUD SPEAKERS AND BULLETIN BOARDS, SILENTLY WAITING FOR NEWS.

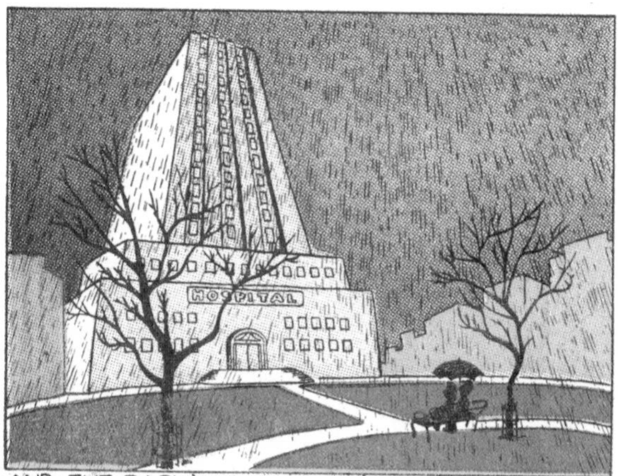

AND THE BABY'S PARENTS KEPT AN ETERNAL VIGIL AS THE FEVER IN THEIR CHILD'S BODY MOUNTED. FINALLY, VERY SUDDENLY AND MYSTERIOUSLY, CAME A TURN FOR THE BETTER.

TO A WEARY AND SLEEPLESS WORLD THE GOOD TIDINGS WENT OUT!

IN CITIES, TOWNS, VILLAGES, AND FARMS-THE NEWS BROUGHT JOY TO MILLIONS OF HEARTS-ACROSS WIDE OCEANS THE WORD WAS FLASHED.

ON SHIPS AT SEA, ON ICEBERGS NEAR THE NORTH POLE, AND IN THE DARKEST JUNGLES OF AFRICA, THERE WAS REJOICING.

PEOPLE WHO HAD NOT SMILED FOR YEARS, LAUGHED AND DANCED IN THE STREETS.

AND FINALLY, ONCE AGAIN, ANNOUNCEMENTS WENT OUT TO THE FAR CORNERS OF THE EARTH.

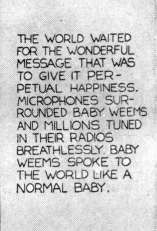

THE WORLD WAITED FOR THE WONDERFUL MESSAGE THAT WAS TO GIVE IT PERPETUAL HAPPINESS. MICROPHONES SURROUNDED BABY WEEMS AND MILLIONS TUNED IN THEIR RADIOS BREATHLESSLY. BABY WEEMS SPOKE TO THE WORLD LIKE A NORMAL BABY.

THE WORLD WAS DUMBFOUNDED! WHAT HAD HAPPENED TO THE GREATEST INTELLECT THE WORLD HAD EVER KNOWN? SPECIALISTS EXAMINED THE BABY ONCE MORE AND SADLY ANNOUNCED THAT THE AMAZING INTELLECT HAD MYSTERIOUSLY DISAPPEARED.

NOBODY COULD UNDERSTAND THESE STRANGE EVENTS—BUT THERE IT WAS—THE WONDER BABY WAS JUST A CUTE BABY. AND SO AS USUAL THE PUBLIC QUICKLY FORGOT ABOUT HIM.

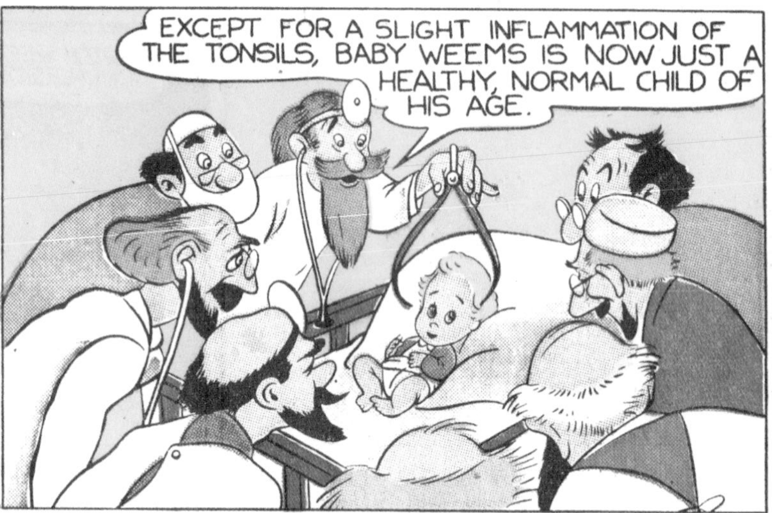

BABY WEEMS WAS NO LONGER NEWS—BUT THOUGH HE HAD FAILED TO BRING HAPPINESS TO THE WORLD, HE DID BRING IT TO HIS OWN FAMILY, WHO UNITED AT LAST, SETTLED DOWN TO PLAIN ORDINARY, LIVING. AND PERHAPS THAT IS HIS GREATEST MESSAGE TO THE WORLD—HE HAS SHOWN US HOW TO ACHIEVE HAPPINESS.

WALT DISNEY'S

FANTASIA

FOREWORD

In making FANTASIA it has been our aim and hope to create a picture that will give pleasure to all types of men, women and children, by appealing to their imagination, humor, the sudden thrill they feel in the presence of beauty, their love of adventure and mystery

Music has something to say to everyone, and every man, woman and child hears a different message, even when listening to the same music, because we all think and feel differently. Some like to close their eyes while listening to music. Others imagine visions of great beauty. To some, music is intellectual—to others, it is emotional. To some, a whole new world of imagination opens up through music.

FANTASIA includes music by Bach, Beethoven, Schubert, Moussorgsky, Tchaikovsky, Dukas, Ponchielli, Stravinsky—all very different kinds of music, and all good of their kind.

Synchronized with this music is an art of color and form in motion, as conceived by one of the most outstanding and creative minds of the world today—Walt Disney His imagination, humor, insight, sense of design and

ability to enter into the life of feeling of any man or animal, tree or stone, and make us feel with him, are the delight of millions of children, and grown-up children, all over the world. He has brought to life a new phase of art—painting in motion. For centuries, painters of all countries of Europe, as well as of China, India, Japan, and Java, have tried to suggest motion in painting. The imagination of Disney, combined with his ever-widening knowledge of recently discovered technical possibilities, has unfolded a new and freely flowing way of painting with color, light, form, and motion.

In making FANTASIA the music has suggested the mood, the coloring, the design, the speed, the character of motion of what is seen on the screen. Disney and all of us who work with him believe that for every beautiful composition there are beautiful pictures. Music by its nature is in constant motion, and this movement can suggest the mood of the picture it invokes.

FANTASIA was created and drawn by artists most of whom have no knowledge of, or training in, music. As enthusiastic listeners, they have been able to penetrate the inner character of the music and discover depths of expression that sometimes have been missed by the musicologists.

Our picture is not presenting the traditional or only possible version. It merely offers one way, out of many possible ways, of visualizing the music, and a way that has been an exciting experience to all of us who contributed to the making of FANTASIA.

Leopold Stokowski

"The Sorcerer's Apprentice" from FANTASIA is presented on the following pages.

ONCE there was a famous sorcerer who lived in a large cave deep in a mountain. Here he mixed magic powders and practiced strange incantations. The walls of his study were lined with books filled with magic formulas. And the sorcerer knew them all by heart.

He could turn a prince into a donkey or —even better—turn a donkey into a prince. He could make the rain go up instead of coming down, and he often did it just to amuse himself.

One afternoon he was bored. He had practiced tricks to pass the time, but it had not been much fun. He glanced up as he saw his helper, the little apprentice, walk wearily by with buckets of water for the big vat in the main chamber. It might be fun to change him into a bird and see what he would do. But as a bird he could not fill the water vat, and that had to be done.

Mickey, the sorcerer's apprentice, set down the two big water buckets and sighed. Then he picked up one bucket, lifted it high and tipped its contents into the huge water vat. Then the second bucket was emptied, and Mickey looked to see how full the vat was.

He groaned! The water was at least two feet from the top. He would have to make many more trips up those long steps to the courtyard where the fountain was and back down again with the full buckets.

Mickey knew that the sorcerer could really fill the water vat just by waving his hand and muttering a few words. But his master said that an apprentice should keep busy, should work hard, before he could even begin to learn how to be a sorcerer. So he made Mickey work day in and day out, carrying water, sweeping and dusting, chopping wood for the fires—even washing dishes.

Mickey thought that such work was not right for someone who was going to learn magic! He should be studying, helping the sorcerer perform his mysterious spells and tricks.

Suddenly Mickey saw a bright flash of green light. He turned and saw that the

sorcerer was doing one of his most difficult tricks. From a flaming green powder, a huge bat had risen into the air. The sorcerer waved his arms and the bat became a beautiful green butterfly. Another gesture and it disappeared in a sparkle of dust.

Mickey was amazed, but the sorcerer seemed only bored. He yawned, took off his hat and put it on the table. Then he crossed the room and mounted the long stairs.

Mickey was alone! He was alone in the cave with all the magic powders and potions and spells, with all the sorcerer's books and—most important of all—with the sorcerer's hat!

It was that pointed hat with the moons and stars on it that held the magic power of the sorcerer. Mickey never before had seen the sorcerer leave it behind him when he went away on one of his rare visits.

So here was the great chance Mickey had been waiting for! Excitedly, even trembling a little bit, he walked to the table and looked at the hat. It looked all right, not at all dangerous.

Mickey reached out his hands and picked up the hat. Nothing happened. Mickey put it on his head. Still nothing happened.

Mickey felt better. He smiled and settled the hat more firmly. It really fit him pretty well. He knew that with the hat on his head he could perform magic.

He was so happy that he danced about the room and hummed a song to himself. Then he saw the broom leaning against the wall. It was just an ordinary broom, but it made Mickey stop and think, it gave him an idea. What a wonderful idea it was! If only it would work!

For just a moment Mickey hesitated. This was much harder than anything he had thought of doing. Still, if he didn't try now, he'd never have another chance like this.

"Here goes!" Mickey said, as he glared at the broom and rolled up his sleeves. He drew back his arms, then threw them forward in a strong movement, pointing straight at the broom. He even wriggled his fingers. But nothing happened. Once more he made the

magic pass with his arms, throwing his whole body into the motion, staring straight at the broom until his eyes almost popped.

Something was happening! The broom began to glow with a strange light, to quiver slightly. Mickey quickly followed up this beginning with another magic pass, and another—and another!

The broom moved! It stood away from the wall by itself! Mickey stared, almost unable to believe that he had succeeded! Just think! Mickey, the little apprentice, was performing a trick just as difficult as any his master ever did! When the sorcerer heard of it he would surely let Mickey stop all that housework and help him in his magic!

But there was more to do before Mickey's plan succeeded completely! He knew he could do it now. He just looked at the broom and commanded it to walk towards him.

The straws of the broom separated in the middle so as to form two short, fat feet. One step forward! Then another. It was not easy, Mickey could see, so he commanded more strongly and the broom waddled forward to him! Then Mickey gave his next command.

From the sides of the broom handle two arms, complete with strong hands, appeared. Then Mickey stepped back and ordered the broom to follow him. He marched out into the main chamber, and the broom obediently followed right at his heels.

Mickey stopped beside that tremendous water vat which, all day long, he had been laboring to fill. There on the floor beside it stood the two water buckets. Mickey motioned to the broom to step between the buckets. He told the broom to pick up the buckets. The broom obeyed every command without a moment's hesitation. Mickey's heart was leaping with joy! Everything was working out just as he had planned. Gaily pointing the way, he stepped across the room towards the long stone stairway leading up to the courtyard. He tripped lightly and happily up the steps that only a short while before had seemed such a hard and tiring climb. Behind him waddled the obedient broom.

When they reached the fountain, Mickey politely pointed and the broom dipped the buckets and filled them. Mickey found that the broom did what he wanted without his having to speak. If he just thought what he desired, the broom obeyed him at once. And best of all, the broom didn't mind a bit. Mickey dancingly led the way downstairs.

The two companions reached the huge water vat in the main chamber of the cave. Mickey just tilted his head a bit and thought the word "pour." The broom emptied the buckets.

Mickey didn't even look to see how full the vat was. With the broom to do the work, why should he care how much more remained to be done? Let the sorcerer build a bigger vat for all he cared! Mickey would just order the broom to fill it up!

Just to make sure that the broom understood clearly, Mickey decided to lead him once more through the routine of his work. Hopping and skipping, he danced up the steps and the broom waddled merrily behind him. To the fountain, down the steps, to the vat! The broom knew its lesson perfectly!

Telling the broom to go on with his task, Mickey sauntered over to the sorcerer's chair, sat down in it happily and put his feet on the table. This was the life a smart apprentice

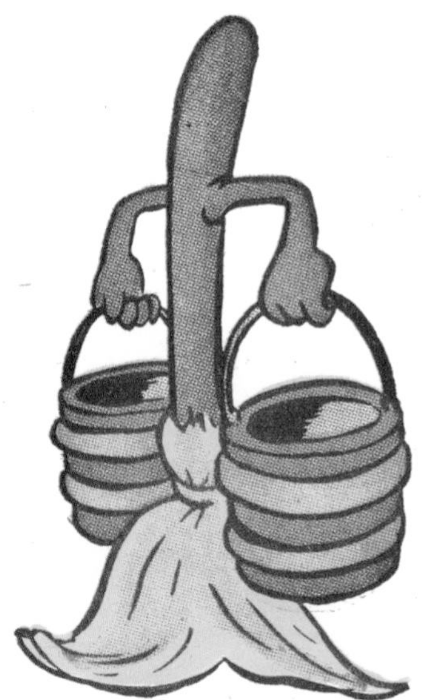

should lead. He could sit here resting comfortably while his broom did all the work.

Mickey watched the broom go up the steps and smiled as he saw it reappear in a few moments, both buckets filled to the brim. He cocked the pointed hat over one ear and settled back as the broom emptied the buckets and started off up the stairs.

Mickey relaxed and sighed. He let his eyelids fall shut, opening them just a crack as the broom swished by with a load of water.

When the vat was filled with water what would he do next? Mickey thought dreamily of the many wonderful spells he would cast, the countless tricks he would perform! He felt sure he could do almost anything in the world. He could float right up through the top of the cave if he wanted to, right up into the sky among the stars.

As he dreamed of it, he suddenly realized that he was floating up into the sky, floating gently and easily upward, farther and farther. He looked about joyously, and saw the stars winking merrily at him. Mickey winked right back at them. This was the best feeling in the world, better even than sitting comfortably while a broom carried water for him. Just wait until the sorcerer heard about this!

Mickey was a little surprised to find himself standing on the top of a high, narrow cliff, so high that it would have made him dizzy if he had not felt so sure of his ability to do anything in the world.

He looked about him and saw a group of planets which formed in line and moved past him. Another group swept past in the other direction. Far off in space he saw a comet flashing its tail at him. He beckoned to it and it obediently swooped in his direction, circled about him, looped and speeded away. He pointed where it should go and it crashed into the group of planets, filling the sky with a shower of sparkling star dust which drifted down slowly.

Mickey watched the flashing particles as they floated down, down, down, far below the towering cliff on which he stood. He was surprised to see that they fell into the ocean, a mighty ocean which surrounded on all sides his narrow cliff of rock. Waves beat against the base of the cliff, first on one side, then the other. Mickey, fascinated, watched the long rolling whitecaps crash against the rocks with a roar. The water splashed high up the cliff.

Mickey decided that it would be a pretty sight if the waves crashed even harder, if the spray splashed even higher. So, with his right arm, he motioned to an oncoming wave, urging it forward.

Mickey turned to the left and motioned to a big wave on that side. Crash! The spray flung itself three-quarters of the way to the top!

Mickey was thrilled and excited. His arm swooped again to the right, again to the left! Each time the waves were higher and stronger. Suddenly one splashed all over him, drenching him from head to foot. He spluttered and coughed and shook himself!

Where was he? The tall cliff was gone. The ocean was gone. But water was all round him as he sat in the sorcerer's chair.

He had been asleep, dreaming those wild dreams of making the comets and planets and waves obey his commands. And all the time the broom had been fetching and dumping water. The vat was overflowing. The water was deep all over the cave! The broom sloshed past him at that moment, on its way toward the stairs to get more water. Frantically, Mickey scrambled after it, grabbing at its arms, grabbing at the buckets. But the broom moved steadily ahead through the water as if nothing in the world could stop it.

Mickey lunged to make a real tackle, tripped over a bench and tumbled headlong into the water. His mouth, his nose, his ears, were

filled with water. Gasping for breath, he came to the surface, looked wildly about him and saw the broom disappearing through the door.

Mickey rushed for the stairs and met the broom coming down, but it brushed him aside as if he were only a bothersome fly.

Mickey grabbed and held tight to one of the buckets. But he couldn't even slow down the determined broom which had been told to fetch and carry water and was obeying that command with the strength that only magic could give him.

Mickey found himself being dragged through the water. Suddenly he was lifted in the air and tossed into the overflowing vat.

He came to the surface and scrambled over the edge of the vat, shouting commands to the broom. But nothing worked. As he raced after the broom, Mickey tried to think of some word which would stop the magic spell. He shouted them all, but the broom went heedlessly up the stairs, on its way to fetch more water.

At the head of the stairs, Mickey saw the axe with which he chopped wood for the sorcerer's fires. In desperation he grabbed it, ran toward the broom at the fountain. It was the only thing to do, so he raised the axe and chopped! Chop! Chop! Chop! The broom fell to the ground broken and splintered in dozens of pieces.

Panting for breath, so tired he could barely move, Mickey slowly walked back to the cave entrance, shutting the door behind him. He leaned against the wall to rest and collect his thoughts.

What was that noise? Mickey turned to listen. Outside in the courtyard there was a sound which seemed to Mickey like that of a broom moving, dipping in the fountain for water. It couldn't be!

Another sound just like the first, and another and another. Fearfully Mickey opened the door and peered into the courtyard. What he saw filled him with terror. Every splinter of the broom had formed itself into a complete new broom, with feet and arms—and buckets! Even as he looked, they started marching toward the door of the cave, row upon row of brooms, each one carrying water.

Mickey slammed the door and braced himself against it. But it was pushed back, and Mickey with it. In marched the brooms knocking Mickey to the ground. He tried to get up! He was knocked down again trampled on by the broom army. Each time he fought to get up, he was thrown to the ground, and the brooms marched over him as they tramped down the steps into the sorcerer's cave.

Inside, the water was way over the top of the vat, over the tables and chairs. It was so high that the last steps were under water. But

the brooms marched straight ahead, through the water, even under the water! They walked to the vat and emptied their buckets. The water rose higher and higher as broom after broom dumped its load.

Mickey ran after them, floundering in the water. Since he had been able to do nothing against just one broom, what hope did he have against this army of brooms? They pushed him aside easily as they walked back up the steps for more water.

The stools and chairs and even the sorcerer's great table were now floating about on the surface of the water. Mickey saw an extra bucket swirling past him. He grabbed it and made frantic efforts to bail out the cave. But where could he throw the water? He slipped and fell again, felt for a footing beneath him and sank below the surface.

Mickey felt that the end had come. As he tried to swim in the rushing waters, grasping at chairs as they whirled near him, he thought only of that dreadful mistake he had made when he thought he could be a sorcerer. If only his master would return!

Something bumped Mickey's head. It was one of the sorcerer's big books, floating on the water. Mickey scrambled on top of it and turned the pages desperately, looking for the spell that could stop this terrible work of the brooms. But the words were printed in a strange language he could not understand. So he just grasped the book tightly as it whirled about on the waters in the cave.

Then Mickey saw the sorcerer—yes, there on the stairs he stood, gazing down at the wild scene below him. His cave was filled with rushing waters, his furniture, equipment and books were floating in a tangled mass on the surface, and his little apprentice was feebly grasping one of the big books. Could even the great and mighty sorcerer do anything in such a terrible situation? Could he do anything without his magic hat, which Mickey felt sure held all the sorcerer's power? That hat, still sat on Mickey's head.

The sorcerer slowly descended the steps, walking majestically, as if he did not know that every step brought him nearer to the deep water in the cave. Would he walk right into the water?

But no—the water backed up! The water moved lower and lower, away from the steps, as the sorcerer stepped down. He did not

even get the soles of his shoes damp! But the waters still swirled over the floor of the cave and Mickey still clutched the book that had saved him. Suddenly the sorcerer raised his arms!

The waters sprang back on either side to make a path across the cave. Mickey was thrown from his book, tossed head over heels into the water. His head cracked against the wall and he fell to the floor.

He was sitting on the floor of the cave, leaning against the wall farthest from the stairway. He looked about, unable to believe his eyes. All the water was gone!

The sorcerer's great table was in its place, and so was the big chair behind it. All the books were sitting on their proper shelves, all the bottles and skulls and equipment of the sorcerer were just where they had been before Mickey started his magic.

Mickey realized what a really great sorcerer his master was. He was filled with admiration to think that all this terrible mess had been completely cleared up in just an instant, with nothing more than a gesture of the arms. And without the magic hat!

Mickey blinked his eyes. There, in the middle of the room, stood the sorcerer, glaring at him angrily.

Slowly Mickey got to his feet and slowly he walked toward the sorcerer, who said not a word but looked so stern that Mickey's heart quaked. Mickey did his best to look ashamed and sorry and humble. He reached up and took from his head the sorcerer's pointed hat. He brushed it and straightened it as best he could before handing it to his master, who took it from him without a word. Why didn't the sorcerer say something, Mickey wondered, or do something?

Then Mickey saw the broom. He stepped over and picked it up, brought it back to the sorcerer who took it and still said nothing. Mickey picked up his two buckets. Perhaps he had better just go ahead with his work.

He started toward the stairs and, as he passed in front of the sorcerer, the broom came down across his seat with a loud whack! Mickey leaped in the air and flew! Never before had the sorcerer's apprentice hurried so fast to fetch water!

OLD MacDONALD DUCK

BRIGHT AND EARLY ONE SPRING MORNING DONALD, THE FARMER, JUMPS OUT OF BED, PUTS ON HIS CLOTHES AND BRUSHES ABOUT THE HOUSE. SUNLIGHT STREAMS THROUGH THE THE WINDOWS, AND THE FRESH SMELL OF A SPRING BREEZE, OF GREEN LEAVES, AND FLOWERS MAKES DONALD HAPPY AS A LARK. AS HE PUTS ON HIS STRAW HAT AND GOES OUTSIDE TO DO THE CHORES, HE SINGS MERRILY. IT'S WONDERFUL TO BE A FARMER, DONALD THINKS, SO CLOSE TO NATURE, TO PLANTS AND FLOWERS, AND ANIMALS.

CLUCK, CLUCK, CLUCK! FOOD!
OINK, OINK, OINK! FOOD!
OINK
OINK
OINK
THE PIGS AND CHICKENS GREET DONALD HAPPILY AND HE SINGS HELLO TO ALL OF THEM.
GOOD MORNING, DEAR CHICKENS, GOOD MORNING TO YOU.
CLUCK, CLUCK, CLUCK
CLUCKETY, CLUCK
"AND ON THAT FARM HE HAD SOME PIGS."
WHERE ARE YOU, MAMA?
OINK! GLUB! OINK!
"EE-EY-EE-EY-OH"
ONLY ONE ANIMAL SEEMS TO BE IN BAD SPIRITS THIS MORNING. THE GOAT DOESN'T APPRECIATE DONALD'S SINGING AT ALL, AND HE MEANS TO SHOW HIM SO.

EE-EY
BAH!
WHOA THERE! EE-EY-EE-EY EE-EY-EE-EY EEEEEEEE! I THOUGHT SONGS WOULD SOOTHE THE SAVAGE BEAST!

AND ON THIS FARM YOU HAVE A GOAT!

EVEN THE UNPLEASANT EXPERIENCE WITH THE GOAT CANNOT DAMPEN DONALD'S SPIRITS.

BUT I ALSO HAVE A FENCE, THANK GOODNESS!

HE CALLS A CHEERY GOODBY TO THE GOAT AS HE SETS OFF TO VISIT HIS FAVORITE, CLEMENTINE, THE COW. HE BOWS LOW AND SAYS "GOOD MORNING CLEMENTINE".

BUT CLEMENTINE JUST SMILES SWEETLY AND GETS READY FOR DONALD TO MILK HER.

OH-OH-A FLY! WATCH OUT, CLEMENTINE!
BZZ
BZZ

SCRAM, BIG BOY- GET OFF OF THERE!

WHEN THE FLY LANDS ON DONALD'S NOSE HE DOESN'T LIKE IT, BUT HE DOESN'T LOSE HIS TEMPER.

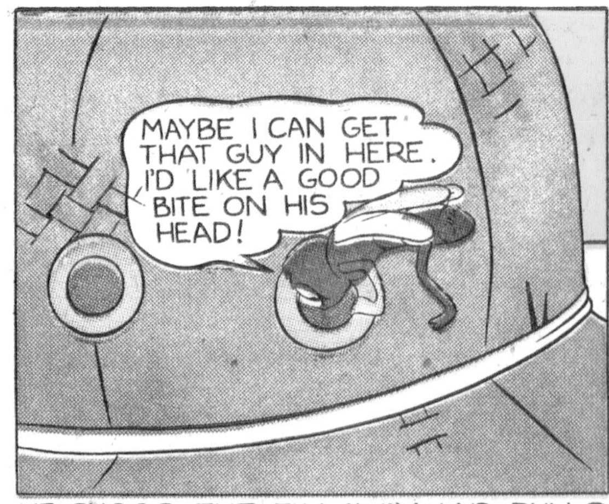

MAYBE I CAN GET THAT GUY IN HERE. I'D LIKE A GOOD BITE ON HIS HEAD!

HE SHOOS THE FLY AWAY AND PULLS HIS HAT DOWN OVER HIS HEAD, BUT THE FLY FINDS THE VENTILATING HOLES IN THE STRAW HAT AND ENTERS.

WELL, I'LL BE-GET OUT OF THERE, YOU DOGGONE PEST! G'WAN! SCRAM!

DONALD RIPS OFF HIS HAT AND SWATS AT THE FLY, SHOUTING AND YELLING FURIOUSLY. THE FLY BUZZES AWAY OUT OF HARM, BUT DONALD IS IN A TERRIBLE STATE BY THIS TIME.

NO FLY IS GOING TO STOP MY MILKING! HERE WE GO, CLEMENTINE.

HE PUTS HIS HAT UNDER THE COW, SITS ON THE MILK PAIL, AND PUTS THE STOOL ON HIS HEAD. THEN HE GOES BACK TO MILKING VIGOROUSLY.

THIS IS A FINE KETTLE OF FISH! WHAT AM I DOING ANYWAY? DOGGONE THAT DOGGONE FLY!
BZZZ. GET TOUGH WITH ME, EH? I'LL FIX HIM! JUST WATCH!

DONALD SEES THE FLY, WHICH IS ABOUT TO ATTACK HIM, TAKES CAREFUL AIM AND SQUIRTS MILK AT HIM.

THE FLY DUCKS INTO AN OLD COFFEE POT AND THINKS HE IS SAFE, BUT DONALD SQUIRTS THE MILK RIGHT DOWN THE SPOUT OF THE POT.

THE POT TIPS OVER AND THE FLY CRAWLS OUT, DRIPPING WITH MILK. IT LOOKS AS IF DONALD HAS WON THE BATTLE.

DONALD IS DELIGHTED AND PLEASED WITH HIMSELF. BUT THE FLY IS ANGRIER THAN EVER. HE DECIDES TO TACKLE THE COW AND MAKE THE COW TAKE CARE OF DONALD.

THE COW THRASHES HER TAIL AT THE FLY, CATCHES DONALD AROUND THE NECK, AND SPINS HIM IN THE AIR.

DONALD LANDS HEAD FIRST IN THE MILK PAIL, BUT CLEMENTINE HELPS HIM OUT. THE FLY GOES BACK TO THE ATTACK.

DONALD AND CLEMENTINE DON'T SEE THE FLY, BUT CLEMENTINE FEELS HIM, ALL RIGHT

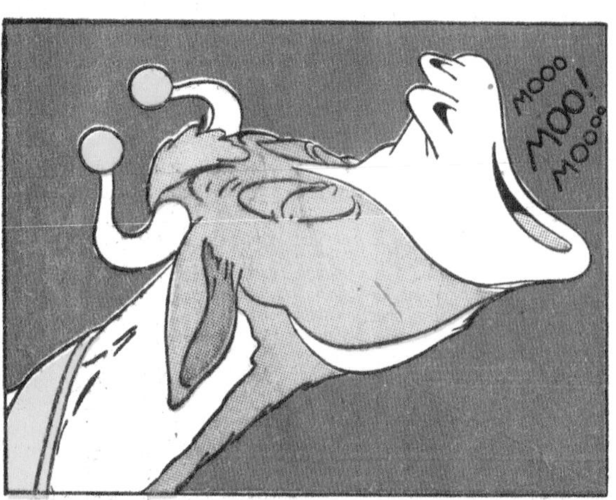

CLEMENTINE HOWLS WITH PAIN, KICKS HIGH IN THE AIR, LASHES HER TAIL, STAMPS AND BELLOWS! DONALD HOLDS ON TO HER TAIL FOR DEAR LIFE, FLYING THROUGH THE AIR AND YELLING!

DONALD IS THROWN LOOSE AND FLIES ACROSS THE BARN. HE CRASHES AGAINST THE WALL WHERE THE HARNESS IS HANGING AND FALLS TO THE FLOOR. FEEDBAG AND COLLAR DRAPE THEMSELVES OVER DONALD, ALMOST DROWNING OUT HIS LOUD ANGRY IMPRECATIONS! CLEMENTINE LICKS HER LEG SOOTHINGLY WHILE THE FLY BUZZES OUT OF THE BARN, HUMMING— "OLD MACDONALD HAD A FARM"

Goofy in "HOW TO RIDE A HORSE"

THE LESSON IN RIDING A HORSE WILL BE CONDUCTED BY THAT EMINENT EQUESTRIAN, GOOFY.

FIRST YOU MUST NOTICE THE RIDING HABIT. THE GREATEST CARE MUST BE TAKEN TO HAVE THE PROPER CUT AND FIT OF ALL THE ARTICLES OF CLOTHING.

OH-OH! LOOK WHAT'S COMING! THIS OUGHT TO BE FUN!

A VERY NECESSARY PART OF RIDING IS THE HORSE ITSELF, ALTHOUGH GOOFY WISHES THAT WERE NOT THE CASE.

THE HORSE WILL SENSE YOUR LACK OF CONFIDENCE AND ACT ACCORDINGLY, WHICH IS TOO BAD.

HAW! HAW! HAW! HAW! HAW!

ER-AH-AHEM! HOW DO YOU DO, I'M SURE! SO GLAD YOU'RE GOING TO HELP ME GIVE THIS RIDING DEMONSTRATION.
SURE, I'LL HELP, ALL RIGHT!
YOU MUST ALWAYS APPROACH THE HORSE WITH A CONFIDENT ATTITUDE. IF YOU DON'T FEEL SO CONFIDENT, TRY TO ACT LIKE IT, THE WAY GOOFY DOES.
I STARTED TO GET ON A HORSE, DIDN'T I? I THINK MAYBE THAT ANIMAL DOESN'T LIKE ME!
BUT SHOULD ANY LITTLE MIS-STEP OCCUR, YOU MUST REGAIN YOUR DIGNITY AT ONCE. THIS IS NOT EASY!
DAD-GUM IT! MAYBE A CARROT WILL WIN HIM OVER
SO HE'S TRYING TO BRIBE ME NOW!

A HORSE WILL BECOME YOUR FRIEND IF YOU OFFER HIM SOME MORSEL OF FOOD HE LIKES, BUT CARE MUST BE TAKEN NOT TO LET HIM GET TOO FRIENDLY.

YOU MUST BE A STRICT DISCIPLINARIAN WITH A DIFFICULT HORSE SO THAT HE WILL BECOME OBEDIENT TO EVERY COMMAND YOU GIVE HIM.

THE MINUTE A HORSE BECOMES TOO INTIMATE WITH YOU, HE WILL TAKE ADVANTAGE OF YOUR KINDNESS.

LIKE A SPOILED CHILD THE SPOILED HORSE WILL WALK ALL OVER YOU, IF YOU LET HIM.

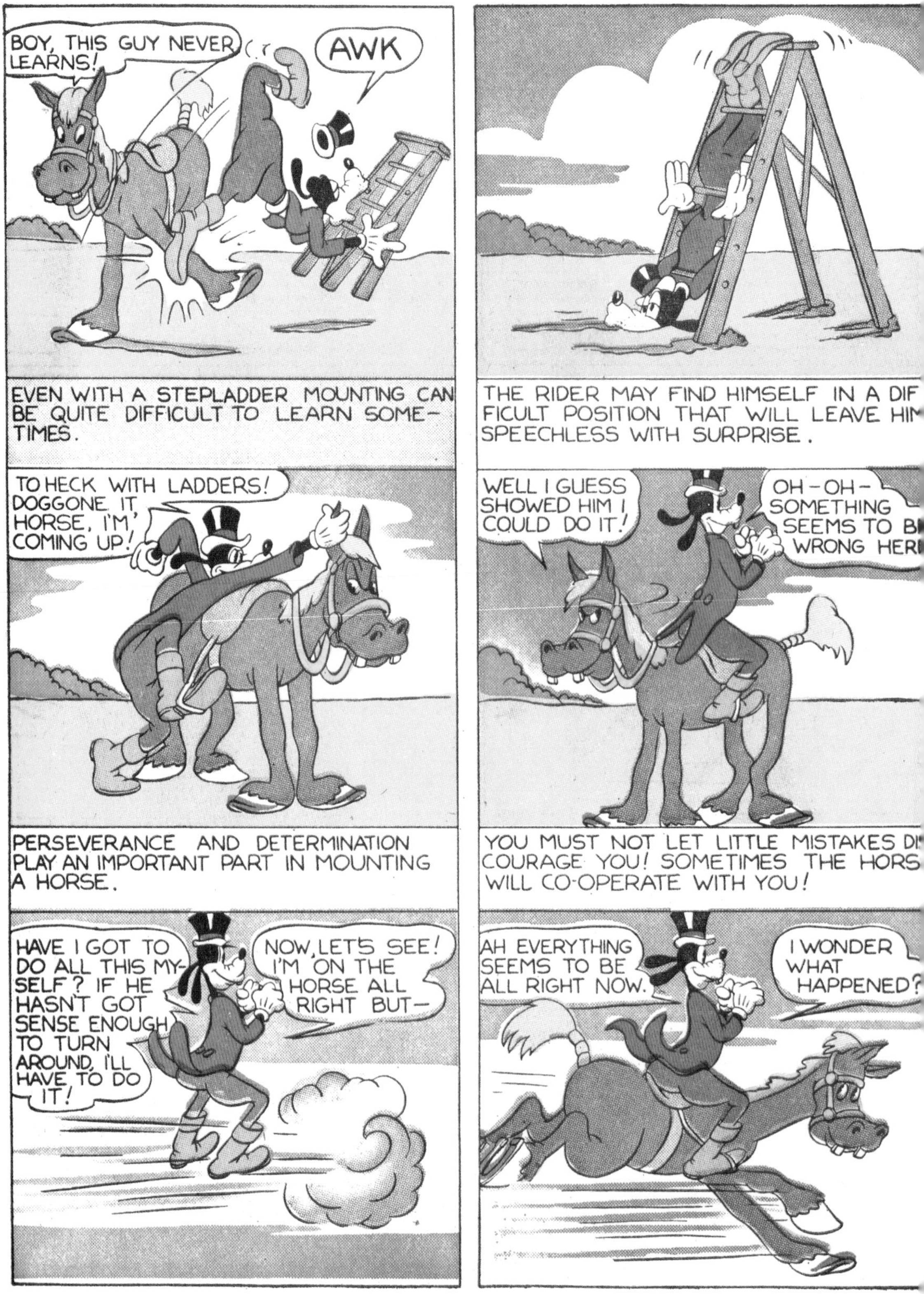

BOY, THIS GUY NEVER LEARNS!
AWK

EVEN WITH A STEPLADDER MOUNTING CAN BE QUITE DIFFICULT TO LEARN SOME-TIMES.

THE RIDER MAY FIND HIMSELF IN A DIF FICULT POSITION THAT WILL LEAVE HIM SPEECHLESS WITH SURPRISE.

TO HECK WITH LADDERS! DOGGONE IT, HORSE, I'M COMING UP!

PERSEVERANCE AND DETERMINATION PLAY AN IMPORTANT PART IN MOUNTING A HORSE.

YOU MUST NOT LET LITTLE MISTAKES DI COURAGE YOU! SOMETIMES THE HORS WILL CO-OPERATE WITH YOU!

HAVE I GOT TO DO ALL THIS MY-SELF? IF HE HASN'T GOT SENSE ENOUGH TO TURN AROUND, I'LL HAVE TO DO IT!
NOW, LET'S SEE! I'M ON THE HORSE ALL RIGHT BUT—

OH BOY! OH BOY! LOOK AT ME! I'M REALLY RIDING A HORSE

ALL WELL-TRAINED SADDLE HORSES HAVE DIFFERENT GAITS. FIRST, THE GENTLE MOTION OF THE TROT- NEXT THE MORE SPIRITED GALLOP.

THE IMPORTANT THING IS TO STAY WITH YOUR HORSE - IF POSSIBLE. BUT IF YOU FALL, BE DETERMINED TO TRY AGAIN.

NO, SIR, I'M NOT GOIN' OVER THAT BIG LOG

THE SUDDEN BURST OF SPEED MAY TAKE YOUR BREATH AWAY AND MAYBE THE HORSE TOO! BUT IF YOU KEEP YOUR HEAD - AND SEAT - YOU'LL BE ALL RIGHT
BOY, I'M GETTIN GOOD! I'M GOIN' TO DO THIS RIGHT THIS TIME!
OH YEAH?
THE NEXT DEMONSTRATION WILL BE IN JUMPING. THE HORSE MAY BE A LITTLE OBSTINATE, BUT THE RIDER MUST BE FORCEFUL ABOUT IT!
LISTEN, NOW, JUMP! COME ON, HORSIE, PLEASE JUMP!
NO

AT THE END OF A LOVELY DAY OF RIDING YOU WILL TURN HOME RELUCTANTLY.

BUT THE HORSE MAY NOT BE QUITE SO RELUCTANT TO GO HOME.

IN FACT, HE MAY JOG ALONG AT QUITE A MERRY CLIP WHEN HE THINKS OF HIS FOOD AND HIS WARM STALL, AS GOOFY SOON LEARNS.

GOOFY IS NOT FAR BEHIND, BUT JUST FAR ENOUGH TO MAKE A SLIGHT DIFFERENCE TO HIM. WHEN IT IS ALL OVER, THE HORSE IS QUITE HAPPY ABOUT THE WHOLE THING. FOR HIM THE DEMONSTRATION HAS BEEN A GREAT SUCCESS. HE FEELS SURE HE HAS TAUGHT YOU A GOOD MANY LESSONS ABOUT HORSEBACK RIDING.

GOOFY IS NOT SO SURE HE CAME TO TEACH YOU TO RIDE, BUT HIS LATEST ADVICE IS TO FORGET THE WHOLE THING AND TAKE UP TIDDLEDYWINKS AS A SPORT.

4. Frances Gifford shows Robert Benchley a painting on a "cel" in the inking department of the Disney studios. The figure of the little deer is painted on transparent cellophane before being photographed.

After many exciting and some embarrassing adventures in the Disney Studios, Robert Benchley finally reaches Walt's office. Walt takes Benchley to a projection room, where they see the latest Disney film, just completed. It is—of course—"The Reluctant Dragon."

6. This monster machine is the famous multiplane camera which was developed in the Disney Studios. Here the millions of tiny pictures making up a Disney movie are taken. In "The Reluctant Dragon," the camera becomes the star performer of one scene in which it almost scares Robert Benchley out of his wits.

YA DOGGONE KIDS MUST HAVE BUBBLES ON THE BRAIN! HERE-- GIMME THOSE!
AND DON'T LET ME CATCH YA BLOWIN' 'EM AGAIN!
WE'RE NOT
BLOWIN' BUBBLES,
UNCA DONALD!
4TH AVE.
B. ST.
?
YA DOGGONE KIDS MUST HAVE BUBBLES ON THE BRAIN! HERE-- GIMME THOSE!
AND DON'T LET ME CATCH YA BLOWIN' 'EM AGAIN!

THE LEGACY OF AL TALIAFERRO

Carl Barks' work on Donald Duck and Uncle Scrooge has made him a legend among comic book aficionados. But if Barks is the definitive Duck artist in comic books, Al Taliaferro must be considered the master of the Donald Duck comic strip. He was the first to adapt the screen duck for comics and drew the strip from its inception in 1936 until his death in 1969. Except for Mickey Mouse cartoonist Floyd Gottfredson, no other Disney comic strip artist had so long a tenure or defined a character so completely.

Taliaferro was born in Montrose, Colorado, in 1905 and moved to California in 1918, settling in Glendale. After studying at the California Art Institute, he began his career at the Disney Studio on January 5, 1931. His first published work was inking Gottfredson's Mickey Mouse Sunday page (from January 17, 1932 to late in that year). Then, in 1933, he took over penciling and inking the *Silly Symphonies* Sunday strip, adapting such classic cartoons as "Bugs in Love," "Elmer Elephant," and "The Three Little Pigs."

Most important was his adaptation of "The Wise Little Hen." The first page of this story, dated September 16, 1934, contained the initial comic strip appearance of a minor character who would become a Disney superstar: Donald Duck. At first Donald was an ungainly figure, long-necked and long-billed, but his personality—and refinements in his appearance—quickly made him a rival to Mickey's stardom. His popularity was rewarded with a special Silly Symphonies strip "Featuring Donald Duck," which began on August 30, 1936. This was the first comic strip to feature Donald as a lead character. On August 22, 1937, the Silly Symphonies logo was dropped, and for the duration of Donald's appearance, Donald Duck became the strip's title.

Donald Duck in "The Wise Little Hen" (1934), written by Ted Osborne and illustrated by Al Taliaferro

At first Taliaferro followed the cartoons in casting Donald as a mischievous prankster, more child than adult. Soon, however, he decided to break new ground. He suggested that the Studio create three nephews for Donald and feature them in a short. The idea was accepted, and in February 1937, the story department sent Taliaferro a memo congratulating him on inventing the new family members. The ducklings debuted in Taliaferro's Sunday page on October 17 of that year. This strip, which contains the first mention of the boys' mother, also provides a reason why they are living with their uncle. A letter explains that cousin Della has left them with Donald while their father recuperates in the hospital, a victim of their prank with a firecracker. For their film appearance in "Donald's Nephews," the letter was shortened to a postcard and Della's name changed to Dumbella, but the basic explanation remained.

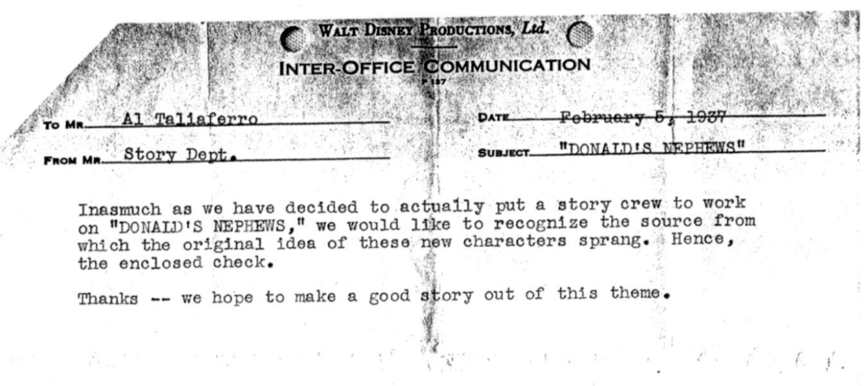

WALT DISNEY PRODUCTIONS, Ltd.

INTER-OFFICE COMMUNICATION

TO MR. Al Taliaferro DATE February 5, 1937

FROM MR. Story Dept. SUBJECT "DONALD'S NEPHEWS"

Inasmuch as we have decided to actually put a story crew to work on "DONALD'S NEPHEWS," we would like to recognize the source from which the original idea of these new characters sprang. Hence, the enclosed check.

Thanks -- we hope to make a good story out of this theme.

Floyd Gottfredson would later recall that "when Al introduced the duck nephews, he did it emulating the three nephews in [the] *Happy Hooligan* [comic strip] that [F. W.] Opper had done. Hooligan had three nephews that were all identical." Dana Coty, a gag man who later sold story ideas to Carl Barks for his comic book tales, came up with the euphonious names, Huey, Dewey, and Louie, with the names taken from Huey Long, governor of and later senator from Louisiana; Thomas Dewey, governor of New York and subsequent presidential candidate; and Louis Schmitt, an animator at the Disney Studio in the 1930s and 1940s.

Additional inspiration for the nephews may have been sown as early 1932, when Taliaferro inked the first appearance of Morty and Ferdie Fieldmouse in the Mickey Sunday page (September 18). Like Huey, Dewey and Louie, Mickey's nephews were mischief-makers, and from their first meeting with Donald on March 31, 1935, they enjoyed tormenting him. Mrs. Lucy Yarrick, Taliaferro's widow, has confirmed the influence, adding that her husband gave Donald three nephews in hopes of creating even more gags than the mouse twins provided. Further inspiration for the duck triplets came in 1936, when Taliaferro adapted two cartoons for the Sunday pages: "The Further Adventures of the Three Little Pigs" and "The Practical Pig." In both stories, the Big Bad Wolf is abetted by three small but ravenous sons. Taliaferro felt that making the Ducks a family would add domestic complications to the already rich gag possibilities.

It was an inspired idea. By giving Donald boys of his own, Taliaferro transformed the duck from a childish prankster to a parent who was still so immature that his victimization by his foster children became doubly funny. Making them nephews allowed Donald to remain a bachelor. It also toned down the boys'

disobedience: behavior that could be excused in distant relations would never be tolerated in sons. In the five Sundays following their initial appearance, the nephews drove Donald into a fury.

Taliaferro may have felt that they were too antagonistic, and on November 22, 1937, he jettisoned them from the strip. They are recalled home to their mother, but go only after a ferocious battle with Donald, no doubt wanting to stay to inflict further abuse. They would not return until February 25, 1940, after a new, regular Donald Sunday strip had been launched and Taliaferro had mellowed their characters considerably.

The Donald Sunday feature ended its run in *Silly Symphonies* on December 5, 1937. The strip might have stayed in limbo, except for Taliaferro's belief that the duck should have a permanent strip of his own. He approached Walt Disney with the idea, and a Donald Duck daily strip was born in the *Pasadena Star-News* on February 7, 1938. It was followed on December 10, 1939, by the debut of a new Donald Sunday page. Both were the product of a collaboration between Taliaferro and gag writer Bob Karp, a team which would last over thirty years.

Donald's Saint Bernard, Bolivar (1939), written by Bob Karp and illustrated by Al Taliaferro

Inspired by having his own strip, Taliaferro began creating more new characters, drawing on his daily life. On March 17, 1938, he presented Donald with a huge, bounding Saint Bernard named Bolivar, whose misadventures were based on the real-life escapades of Taliaferro's Scottish terrier George McTavish. Bolivar soon became the Duck family dog, and even turned up years later in several of Carl Barks' ten-page Donald stories. His name was later changed to Bernie in the strip, and—temporarily—Bornworthy in the comics, when the Studio received a complaint from the Bolivian government, which felt that the dog mocked their national hero Simon Bolivar. Much later, emotions cooled, as Donald's pet regained his original name from 1992 to the present day.

The simplest domestic events would often spark a gag. When Lucy came home with a new hat, Al would get revenge by drawing a caricature of her chapeau on Daisy or a comically fat woman.

"Once I put my own telephone number in a strip about Donald's delivery service," Taliaferro recalled. "I received so many calls the day it was printed that I finally had to take the phone off the hook." As a perverse testimony to the strip's popularity, people quacked into the receiver.

Truest to life was Grandma Duck. Her humorously unsettling sojourns with Donald were inspired by visits from Taliaferro's mother-in-law, who would come to help care for Lucy's newborn children. Described by Lucy as "small but mighty," Mrs. Donnie Wheaton was a traditionalist who lived on a farm. In the strip, she became matriarch of the Duck clan; along with Mrs. Wheaton's old-fashioned virtues, Grandma Duck even has her hairdo. Grandma first appeared as a portrait painting in the Sunday strip for August 11, 1940, shortly before Mrs. Wheaton became a grandmother. The character herself walked into the daily strip on September 27, 1943, just one week after the birth of Taliaferro's son William, and the first thing she did was scrub Donald's neck. Her presence not only made the Ducks a more complete family, it made Donald himself subject to an authoritarian parent.

Until Carl Barks began creating original stories for the comic books, Taliaferro's work offered the definitive portrait of Donald. Later the two versions would coexist, each supreme in its own medium. But it was Taliaferro who created the Duck pantheon and established the elements upon which Barks and subsequent Disney artists would draw.

—Thomas Andrae

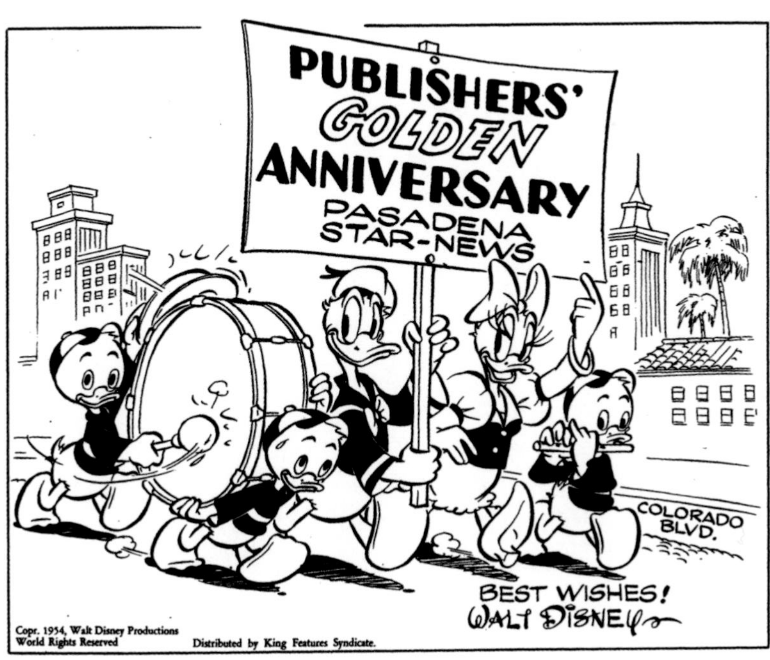

Taliaferro's mature postwar designs for Donald and the gang. Promotional art, 1954.

These six strips present the first appearance of Huey, Dewey and Louie, appearing in the *Donald Duck* Sunday newspaper strips in 1937. Plot and art by Al Taliaferro; script by Ted Osborne.

DONALD DUCK.
by WALT DISNEY
HI, DONALD HOW'S YER NEPHEWS?
?
!
?
SO!! HIDING!
HELLO, UNCA DONALD!
!
QUACK QUACK QUACK QUACK !!!!
DONALD DUCK.
by WALT DISNEY
URK!
?
?
CRASH!
SO!
WALT DISNEY

DONALD DUCK
by WALT DISNEY
CRASH!
CRASH!
BREAK MY WINDOWS, WILL YOU?
DONALD DUCK
by WALT DISNEY
WHOM
RING!
TELEGRAM FOR YOU, UNCA DONALD!
IT'S FROM YOUR MA! SHE WANTS YOU TO COME BACK HOME!
WAAAAAAA! WE WANT TO STAY HERE! WE DON'T WANNA GO HOME!
OH! YOU DON'T, DON'TCHA?
WALT DISNEY

SEE, UNCA DONALD, IT'S CAUGHT IN THE TREE!
YA DOGGONE
DS MUST HAVE
UBBLES ON THE
BRAIN! HERE--
GIMME THOSE!
AND DON'T LET ME CATCH YA BLOWIN' 'EM AGAIN!
WE'RE NOT
BLOWIN' BUBBLES,
UNCA DONALD!
4TH AVE.
B. ST.
SHUC
--ONE M
WON'T
ME
?
?
AND DON'T LET ME CATCH YA BLOWIN' 'EM AGAIN!

About the Authors

CARL BARKS has become synonymous with the gold standard of Disney Comics, having created some of the best-loved Disney Duck characters and stories of all time. Creator of such endearing characters as Uncle Scrooge, the Beagle Boys, Gyro Gearloose and many others, Barks is largely responsible for the world of the Ducks as we know it. His legacy is inestimable, and his stories continue to enjoy success with modern audiences.

BOB KARP began work at the Walt Disney Studio in character modeling, but moved on to write an astounding 36 years of *Donald Duck* newspaper strips with Al Taliaferro and then Frank Grundeen. He also collaborated with his brother Lynn on the syndicated comic strip "The Middles."

JACK HANNAH produced art for many *Donald Duck* comic strips in the mid-1940s, though he's perhaps best known for his work with the Disney Animation Studio. An animator, storyman and director, Hannah directed 95 films over the course of his career featuring Mickey Mouse, Donald Duck, Chip 'n' Dale and many others. He also spent several years as leader of the California Institute of the Arts' Character Animation program.

AL TALIAFERRO is renowned for his 31-year stint drawing the *Donald Duck* daily newspaper strips, after successfully lobbying for creation of a daily strip for Donald in the first place. He also worked on a wide range of other Disney characters from Mickey Mouse to Bucky Bug. He is credited with co-creating many enduring characters, such as Huey, Dewey and Louie.

IRVING TRIPP spent an impressive four decades as a comic artist. He produced some of the earliest Disney comic book art starring such characters as Dumbo and the Reluctant Dragon, though Tripp is probably best known for his 38-year stint as inker for the *Little Lulu* comic book. Tripp's varied career also included artwork for Warner Bros., United Features and Little Big Books.

YA DOGGONE KIDS MUST HAVE BUBBLES ON THE BRAIN! HERE-- GIMME THOSE!
AND DON'T LET ME CATCH YA BLOWIN' 'EM AGAIN!
WE'RE NOT
BLOWIN' BUBBLES,
UNCA DONALD!
I GOTTA EAT, BROTHER! I'M A STARVIN' ARTIST!
PORTRAITS PAINTED $2.00
YA DOGGONE KIDS MUST HAVE BUBBLES ON THE BRAIN! HERE-- GIMME THOSE!
AND DON'T LET ME CATCH YA BLOWIN' 'EM AGAIN!